F.A.T.E. 2

Slave Ship from Sergan

Slave Ship from Sergan

A F.A.T.E. Novel

by

Gregory Kern

MEWS BOOKS
LONDON AND CONNECTICUT

Also by Gregory Kern in this series:

F.A.T.E. 1: Galaxy of the Lost.

This work was originally published in the United States of America as
CAP KENNEDY No. 2 SLAVE SHIP FROM SERGAN
Copyright © 1973 by DAW BOOKS, INC.
First published in United States of America by Daw Books, October 1973

*

FIRST MEWS EDITION MAY 1976

*

Mews Books are published by
Mews Books Limited, 20 Bluewater Hill, Westport, Connecticut 06880
and distributed by
New English Library Limited, Barnard's Inn, Holborn, London E.C.1.
Made and printed in Great Britain by Hunt Barnard Printing Ltd., Aylesbury, Bucks.

45200010_6

CHAPTER ONE

From where he stood at the window Elgha Zupreniz could see the undulating surface of the tiny world which was his domain. It was harsh, bleak, an airless scrap of rock circling a dying sun, red light somber on the rounded hills, ruby shadows thick in the vales. Thirty miles long, ten wide and as many deep. Barren, useless, the remnant of a planet which had broken into shards before the beginning of recorded time. His world. His kingdom. His patrimony.

He scowled, great jaws widening, fangs showing blue beneath the emerald of his snarling lips. Eyes, slotted like those of a goat, rested deep beneath brows of massive bone. His crest, sharp with youth, was brightly orange in reflection of his rage. Hands, clawed, gnarled, clenched as he tasted the bitterness of his father's humor.

The old man was dead or he would have spat into his face. Had spat when he had seen him lying in state, his seven brothers in solemn attendance. To them the old fool had given a planet, the lush and fertile world of Obrac. To Elgha he had given a calculated insult. An asteroid on which nothing could grow. A tiny world with no air, no water, nothing but stone and minerals and the too rare gems which alone could command a high price. The gems impossible to obtain without machines and labor.

The thought heightened the anger which stained his crest. A hut, a barely worked mine, equipment which could barely maintain the air he breathed within the flimsy shelter. Some limited stores, primitive tools, broken machinery, and no fuel slugs to power them even if they had been working. His inheritance!

Damn the old fool!

'My lord!' The voice was a soft purr, seeming to caress the window. 'An uncut gem is an ugly thing, but once faceted and polished, it holds a precious beauty. So it is with your domain. To the casual eye it is nothing, a bad joke, an insult even to one such as yourself who grew up accustomed to the rights and privileges of his station. But pause a moment and think, my lord. Your father was not stupid. What chance would you, the youngest, have stood against the selfish greed of your kindred? If he had left you Obrac, how long would it have been before you were challenged?'

Elgha growled deep in his throat. 'Am I afraid of a challenge?'

'Certainly not, my lord. Did I suggest that? But would the fight have been fair? One would have fallen, perhaps more, but all seven?'

Elgha turned from the window, snarling at the hint of weakness. 'Seven and twice seven,' he roared. 'I'd have shredded them all. My brothers and any they chose to send against me.'

Sina Lahari bowed, hiding the mockery in his eyes. Let the big fool rant and roar; no creature of lizard extraction could hope to beat the intelligence of a man. And Sina was a man despite the wild mutations which had peaked his ears and covered his skull and face with mottled fur.

Softly he said, 'And the assassins, my lord? Those who would slip poison into your food and venom into your wine? I have seen the way your brothers look at you behind your back. If you had inherited your father's world, you would have been dead within a week. Not on the floor of honest combat but by stealth and deceit. Your father did not hate you, my lord. He sought to safeguard your life. He knew, as I know and as your brothers must suspect, that your skill and intelligence will enable you to take what he gave and from it make that which will buy you a dozen worlds each as good as Obrac.'

Lies, he thought. The old man had hated the guts of his swaggering, selfish offspring. More than once he had cursed the egg which had given him birth, but it was more than his life was worth to even breathe the truth. Instead he must rely on cunning, flattery, the temptation of great riches. And, when the fool had fallen and the fruit was ripe, the rich harvest would be his.

'Assassins,' breathed Elgha. 'They would dare?'

'Yes, my lord.'

'Against the custom and the traditions of Obrac. My kindred are vile but – assassins?'

The thought shook him and his crest wilted a little, the flaming orange dying to a smoky red. Honest combat he could

6

face, fang against fang, claw against claw, ripping and tearing, feet lifting to disembowel, thumbs gouging at eyes. In the arena he was to be reckoned with, a foe none dared to face, but the subtle threat of assassination was something against which he had no defense.

'It would have been only a matter of time, my lord,' said Lahari, pressing the point. 'But your father saved you from that danger by his gift of this world.'

Elgha snarled, crest brightening as he looked again through the window.

'Think of what those rocks contain. Gems of price which will buy you all you can desire. A softer world for your pleasure, submissive wives, men to obey your every command.'

The snarl showed yet more of the blue fangs. 'You jest, cat-man. Perhaps you forget the anger of the Ghazen. We are not a race to be lightly used. Am I a fool not to believe my eyes? You talk of riches and soft living and bid me to look at barren stone. There are gems within, true, but how to obtain them? With these?' The hands lifted, claws extended. 'Am I a serf to delve in stone? Have I, a noble of Obrac, no pride?'

'Pride and to spare, my lord,' said Lahari quickly.

'You had best remember it.'

'How could I ever forget?'

Elgha rumbled, mollified a little as he turned from the window. Despite his disgusting appearance the cat-man was shrewd and had so far shown himself to be a friend. They had traveled in his ship, lying now on the ground beyond the hut, connected to the flimsy structure by an air-filled tube. And he had been the first with calming words when news of the inheritance had sent Elgha raging through the corridors of the palace.

Words and wine and a whispered plan, never wholly revealed but hinting of great promise. Perhaps too great a promise. The man was a trader, hanging on the fringes of court, bartering goods against favors, the gems wrested from the seas and mountains of Obrac. Few gems, for the Ghazen had no liking for manual labor. To bask in the sun, to drink, to sport in the arena, to follow the warrior-path of tradition was more to their liking. That and pursuing old feuds and maintaining a rigid formality.

Things he had enjoyed, gone now that he owned no land, no farms, nothing to provide the comforts to which he had grown accustomed. He could imagine the sneers when his name was mentioned back at the palace, the grins and shrugs, Elgha Zupreniz – owner of stone.

The thought turned his crest to crimson flame.

'My lord,' said Lahari softly, 'you grow disheartened. There is no need. The jest is on others, not yourself.'

'Explain.'

'I will, my lord. If you will give me the gracious pleasure of your attention?'

He waited as Elgha turned again from the window and crossed the room with heavy tread. He wore glinting mail which covered his own, natural scales, the metal banded with broad straps from which hung dagger and sword, the pouched mass of a missile weapon, the butt shaped to his clawed hand. The bands bore intricate work of beads and stones, the insignia of his rank and visible proof of his prowess. The row of claws hanging in a necklace low on his chest were trophies won in the arena when his bested opponents had chosen to lose a claw instead of their lives. Twelve painted crests showed the fate of those who had once held more courage than sense.

A barbarian, thought Sina Lahari. A creature devoted to the strength of arm and muscle instead of the superior power residing in a human brain. A product of a backward world as yet unaffected by the pulse and tide of true civilization. The member of a static culture which could shatter like glass beneath the right impact. Would shatter, given time.

But before that happened he intended to make his kill.

Luck, he thought. Nothing but pure, unadulterated luck. For years he had hung around the court waiting for his opportunity to present itself. The time when he could move in and collect for all the sneers and abuse he had meekly suffered for the sake of a precarious living. Well, now that was over. Now the opportunity was here. Just play this fool a little, blind him with greed and get him to agree and the thing was as good as done.

Elgha halted before the bench on which he sat. The chipped expanse of cheap plastic which held a few assorted instruments, some graphs, a scale and spectroscope, two soiled plates and a half empty bottle of wine. He caught up the flagon, drained it, set it down with force enough to shatter the glass.

'Speak,' he rumbled. 'My patience grows short.'

'Let us value our assets,' said Lahari quietly. 'I align myself with you, my lord, because in this our aims are one. You agree?'

'A bargain?'

8

'Yes, my lord.' The crest, to Lahari's relief maintained its neutral slate. No anger then if, as yet, no pleasure. Quickly he continued: 'Your world is barren and of no apparent worth as we can both see but, my lord, it need not remain so. There are devices which can seal any workings we care to make, others which will provide air and gravitation. Water can be wrested from the stone and living quarters constructed beneath the surface. These things have often been done. Many societies have their economy based on just such worlds as the one you own.'

Elgha scowled. 'Continue.'

'It requires only the attention of planetary engineers. Such men can be hired. The machines they will need can be bought. Within a short while you will be counting the gems and enjoying what their worth can bring. Think of it, my lord. Your inheritance made to bloom like a flower in the desert. The brothers who now despise you beating their heads in envy.'

An entrancing prospect and one he could enjoy, but harsh reality dulled the pleasure of anticipation. Elgha bared his fangs.

'And the money, you worm? The cash to pay for the hire of engineers? The purchase of machines?'

'That can be arranged, my lord. I have friends. Those who would be willing to invest if the conditions were right. And perhaps you know of those on Obrac who would not be averse to earning easy wealth.'

Every culture everywhere had more than enough of such men.

'A little here, a little there, it adds up, my lord,' said Lahari suggestively. 'And, as I said, I have friends.'

Robbers like himself, thought Elgha. Traders and those who wanted a ready market for dubious goods, cash down and no questions asked. But he had no cash.

Lahari shrugged as he mentioned it.

'My friends can be patient, my lord. For the sake of high profit they will be willing to extend credit. You can leave that to me. All I really require is your sealed authority in order to act on your behalf. You own this world, my lord. You are its sovereign. You have complete power to do exactly as you wish. Let me act for you and you will never regret it.'

Elgha turned and padded back to the window. His crest held the bluish tinge of pleasure, the more pleased he became the brighter it would become. Beyond the pane he saw nothing he had not seen before but, spurred by his imagination, he could visualize huts, shafts, domes to seal in air, pumps to distribute water, mounds of detritus, tunnels probing deep, and gems, a mountain of gems.

The workers would find them. The creatures who would delve and sift and win the stones from where they lay.

The workers!

Men could be hired for short engagements. Machines brought on credit to be paid for when they had earned their cost. But the people who would do the actual work would need high wages and regular recreation. Food, water, baths, medical facilities, transportation.

His shoulders sagged.

The dream was over, dead before it had kicked itself into life. Unless . . . ?

'You have nothing to worry about, my lord,' said Lahari softly. Almost it seemed as if he had read the other's thoughts. 'Everything can be arranged.'

'Everything?'

'Indeed, yes, my lord.'

Elgha Zupreniz wanted to believe that. He wanted to be rich and envied and to gloat over those who basked in the sunlight of their home world. His brothers, their associates, those who now considered him a joke. And if the trader could manage it – why not?

What had he to lose?

'You need my sealed authority, you say?'

'Indeed yes, my lord.' Lahari's bow hid the triumph in his eyes. The fish was hooked, the bait swallowed, now to make sure of the harvest. 'A declaration making me your agent able to act and deal on your behalf. My friends – ' He broke off, shrugging, spreading his hands. 'I am but a trader, my lord. My word is good but, in business, more is needed. The power of a king. The protection of the ruler of a world. Elgha Zupreniz, Lord of – ' He hesitated. 'Sergan? You like the name, my lord?'

Sergan. It had a roll, a feel of the tongue, a name with connotations of power. Elgha Zupreniz swelled a little, his crest shining blue. Lord of Sergan! A title fit for a man of pride. And if his world was only a scrap of rock drifting around a dying sun, who would know? And, once the gems provided the wealth he craved, who would care?

His hand lifted, the light gleaming from the extended claws, and Lahari cringed as they reached toward his face. But there was no menace in the gesture. He felt the touch of the claws, needle points indenting his fur, and heard the booming voice as Elgha made his decision.

'As you have promised, so shall it be. From this moment on, you are my agent, my arm and my voice, my hand and my eye. Now rise, Sina Lahari, Baron of Sergan. You have much to do.'

The jackpot, thought Lahari as he made the ritual gesture of obedience demanded by Ghazen formality. Real authority under the genuine ruler of a genuine world. In two years, three at the most, his fortune would be made.

CHAPTER TWO

The captain of the *Meeresh* was sorry to see him go.

'It was fun, Cap. It isn't often I get the chance of decent company in this part of the galaxy. Too many routine jobs and too much aggravation with petty details. You certain that you wouldn't like to sign on as second officer?'

Kennedy smiled and shook his head.

'A cut of the profit and a guaranteed salary? No?' The captain stuck out his hand. 'Well, I guess you know what you want, but if you should change your mind the offer will still be there. In the meantime, good luck and plenty of it.'

'Full holds and high returns.' Kennedy closed his fingers around the captain's hand as he gave the traditional farewell common among those plying for trade between the stars.

'Watch the streets,' warned the captain as he turned to leave. 'Tulgol is a rough world.'

In this part of space most worlds were, with cities like jungles and houses close-shuttered at the approach of night. Kennedy left the spacefield, long legs carrying past the fence, the lounging watchers, the whispered invitation of lurking touts.

'Long trip, mister? Want a little fun?'

'Good food, soft beds, company if you want it.'

11

'Double your pay at an honest table.'

'Try the Double Moon for fast and exciting action. You want a guide?'

'No.'

'You sure, mister?' The tout pressed close, a hand falling on Kennedy's arm. 'Don't miss the chance while you've got it.'

Kennedy looked down at the thin face, the bleared eyes, and slack mouth. Coldly he said, 'I'll give you one chance. Take your paw off my arm or I'll break your neck.'

For a moment the tout looked into the hard face, the bleak eyes, then hastily dropped his hand, backing, his voice a whine.

'No offense, mister. Just trying to be helpful. There's no need to get rough.'

Kennedy pressed on, past the area of light fringing the field, the assembled loungers, heading toward a maze of narrow streets and alleyways. It was an apparently foolish thing to do, no normal man would wander at night in the sleazy streets of Tulgol, but Kennedy was in a hurry and he was no ordinary man.

Even as he walked his ears were alert with instinctive caution, eyes darting from side to side, noting the lamp suspended over the gaping maw of an alley, a door which closed as he approached, a shadow which drifted from a spot ahead to seemingly vanish in thin air.

The nocturnal life to be expected in such a place. Like most worlds of its kind, Tulgol changed when the sun lowered beneath the horizon. Then honest men stayed snug at home or stuck to the brilliantly lit main streets, carried in powered vehicles, sometimes attended by armed guards. Even then they stayed clear of the alleys and narrow paths barely lit, if lit at all, with the stars glimmering between the tops of buildings which almost touched as they leaned at crazy angles. Only the sector devoted to synthetic joy blazed with light and careless life, a host of taverns and places of entertainment pandering to those jaded after long flights through the bleak emptiness of space, or to others, less bored, but with greater appetites. The rich traders and transients, the younger sons and daughters of established merchants stealing out from shuttered dwellings to taste forbidden fruits.

In such a place Kennedy would have been safe – aside from the harpies who would have tried to rob him in barely disguised ways. But here, in these dark and winding alleys, lurked a kind

12

of life peculiar to civilized worlds. Men who emerged with the dark, thinking animals more ruthless than any natural beast of prey. Desperate, some of them, driven to scavenge what they could in order to stay alive. Others, less desperate, dealing in mutilation and death for the sake of easy money or the simple venting of their drug-crazed passions.

A hard world here on the edge of the civilized portion of the galaxy, where only the strong could hope to survive and where there was no place for the weak and gentle.

Kennedy had been in such places before and was well-suited to the environment. Beneath the somber black of his tunic and pants, the ebon hue edged with gold, his muscles bunched and smoothed with a trained economy of movement. Above wide shoulders rose the column of his neck, the hard determination of his jaw, the eyes set beneath level brows. His ears were small, clinging tightly to his scalp, and his mouth, edged with lines of humor, could become cruel.

He heard a soft rustle of movement, the scrape of a boot against stone, the quick inhalation of indrawn breath coming from somewhere behind. Without altering his rapid pace he aimed for the center of an opening filled with a soft luminescence. The glow came from lanterns suspended behind tinted panes of crystal, filling the darkness with patches of molten color, red, green, blue, flaming amber, and somber brown, shadows linking thick between the patches of light.

Again came the soft sound of furtive movement, the patter of running feet, the boots wreathed in muffling rags, the panting of breath sucked into shriveled lungs. Kennedy did not turn his head, trusting to his senses to localize the noise. Behind, naturally, about thirty yards and to his right. If the man should make a rush, there would be plenty of time to turn and deal with whoever it was. The greater danger lay ahead where the soft luminescence died and gave way to a darkness deeper by comparison with the light.

The alley opened there, a small plaza giving on to other alleys, one of which he would take.

As he reached the opening, a whistle came from his right. It was low, a ghostly warble, fluting as if made by a night bird. It was repeated from a point ahead, from within the alley he intended to take. A cautious man, disturbed, a little afraid, would have instinctively turned to his left away from the enig-

13

matic sounds. That was the plan of those who lurked in the darkness.

They did not know their man.

Kennedy strode along the path he intended to take, ears alert, eyes strained as he stared into the darkness. He had good night-vision. He saw the shape against a wall, the arm raising, the club it held a vicious mass weighed with lead. Before it could fall he had darted forward, left fist clenched and driving forward, right hand raised to grip the weapon. He felt the softness of a stomach beneath his clenched knuckles, the gush of fetid air as the man doubled; then the club was in his hand, lifting, falling to crush the skull.

As the man fell, Kennedy turned and ran toward shapes advancing from the darkness.

He caught the glimpse of a face in the glow from the luminescent alley, the uplifted hand, the metal of a gun clutched in the fingers. The club whined as it hurtled through the air, hitting the pale face with a soggy impact, turning the nose, the mouth into a mask of blood.

A man called out, 'Karn!'

Another, deeper voice, snarled, 'Never mind him, you fool! Get the mark!'

Two of them at least. Add the one who had followed him, the one who had whistled, and Kennedy knew that he faced four men at least. The whistler would be at his rear, the one who had followed at his left. They could be armed with missile weapons, lasers, perhaps, clubs and knives certainly. If he waited they would gang up, move in familiar concert, close in for the kill, more vicious now that he had taken toll of their number.

Kennedy gave them no chance.

Even as the club left his hand he was lunging forward as his agile mind evaluated the situation. The man who had held the gun was doubled, hands to his smashed face, coughing and crying with shock and pain. He could wait. Two others, near-shadows in the darkness, could not. Before they knew it, Kennedy was between them, hands stiffened, the hard edges of his palms trained instruments of violent destruction.

He struck, felt cartilage yield, hit once more to complete the ruin of throat and neck. He sprang aside from the man, dead but not yet fallen, catching the glimmer of steel as a blade lanced toward his stomach. The point touched his shirt, then he had trapped the wrist, his right foot rising in a vicious kick. As the man shrieked and slumped, Kennedy twisted the trapped wrist, felt the snap of bone and jumped backward as a club whined through the space where his head had been.

The man who had followed him along the alleys, almost soundless on his muffled boots, his face open, gaping as he tried to regain his balance. The soft light from the shining passage revealed a blotched and scarred face, tangled hair, eyes insane with curious hatred. Their light died as Kennedy slashed the edge of his right hand at the back of the neck in a spine-snapping chop.

Three dead and two injured, but the man with the battered face had held a gun and he could still use it. Kennedy kept moving, dancing on the balls of his feet, eyes searching the darkness. He saw the gun, the hand reaching toward it, the blood-smeared mask and glaring eyes. As the weapon lifted, he jumped forward, gripped the wrist, lifted as his right struck at a vulnerable point. From somewhere behind he heard the quick patter of running feet, the harsh sounds of a man straining legs and lungs to the limit of their capacity.

The final man, running, terrified at the price his companions had paid for their nocturnal adventure.

Coldly Kennedy looked at the carnage. He felt no remorse, pity, or regret for what he had done. These men would have killed him, stripped his body and perhaps have left him crippled and maimed, blinded, even, unable to do more than lie helpless, whimpering with agony. He had seen such things before, the helpless victims of roving gangs left as a ghastly token of their successful hunt.

'Mister!' The voice was a thread of pain. 'For God's sake, mister!'

The injured man, risen now, his unbroken arm hanging so as to nurse his stomach. Kennedy frowned. The man should have been unable to rise; the kick he had delivered must have missed its target by an inch. That or the man had worn protection.

'Please, mister!' The voice rose as Kennedy stepped forward. 'I didn't know. They told me it was just a snatch. A rap on the head and that was all. That was all we intended. I swear it!'

Kennedy lifted his hand. The thing was vermin and vermin should be exterminated.

'For God's sake!' The voice rose to a scream. 'Don't look at me like that! I tell you we meant no real harm. I – please, mister. Don't kill me! Don't!'

The plea of a creature who wanted to live. Who wanted to walk in the sun and smell the air and see the riotous colors of sunrise and sunset. Who now faced death, cold, efficient and deserved.

On his knees the man said, 'I was starving. No berth, no work, nothing to hope for. They wanted an extra man. Just a snatch job, they said. Nothing to it. No harm intended. You owed money and the boss wanted to see you. That was all. Please, mister. I didn't know they carried guns. Karn said –'

'Karn?'

'That one. The one with the gun. He was the boss. I was to get ten crelten for helping out.'

'Who said they wanted to see me?'

'I don't know.'

'Don't lie to me!' Kennedy loomed over the kneeling man, his face like stone even while a part of his awareness listened for any sign of further danger. 'You couldn't know that Karn wouldn't get hurt. What would happen then?'

'I don't know,' said the man again. 'Honest, mister, I just don't know. There were others –' He glanced to where they lay, untidy heaps against the stone. 'Maybe they would have known, but I didn't. I was just a pair of hands.'

A pair of hands and a knife which he had been willing to use. Had tried to use.

The man cried out as he saw the face, the hard eyes, the cruel twist of the mouth. He was looking at jury, judge, and executioner and knew it. At that moment Kennedy was something more than human. He was a man who hated wanton violence, who had dedicated his life to the protection of the weak and the establishment of decent conditions for all. To him the kneeling creature was degraded filth, a thing to be destroyed without qualm or compunction.

There was only one way in which the man could save his life.

'Talk,' rapped Kennedy. 'Tell me why I was hunted and why I was wanted. I want to know who employed you and why. Where I was to be taken if overpowered. Talk, damn you! Talk!'

He sensed rather than heard the soft impact of a boot set cautiously on stone. At once he was moving, jumping backward, turning in the air to face the sound. Fire spat from the shadowed alley, a thread of flame which reached like a probing finger, not toward him but toward the kneeling man.

Flame burst from his chest, the explosion ripping open his torso and shredding his lungs, flinging him backward to lie with blank eyes and a mouth which, though open, would never speak again.

Before the echoes died, Kennedy had moved, darting from where he stood, stooping, snatching up the gun from where it lay beside the man who had tried to use it and who had died trying. Tense against the protection of a wall, he waited, eyes probing the darkness, finger hard against the trigger.

He heard the pad of a boot, a rasp as if something metallic had touched against stone. He fired, rolled, fired again. Flame blossomed from two points down the alley. He heard a cry, a gasp of pain, and then the sound of running feet.

He rose, waiting, listening, but there was nothing more. Only the soft light from the luminescent windows like a pale rainbow in the night. The gleam of distant stars overhead. The dead lying where they had fallen, mute testimony to the ruthless efficiency of the man they had tried to take.

CHAPTER THREE

The door was set deep in a mouth of stone, a panel of solid wood strapped with iron, a judas window grilled with thick bars. Kennedy rapped the muzzle of the gun he had taken against the wood, waited, repeated the signal. Light streamed from above, showing the open maw of the window, the mirror inside, the face reflected on the surface.

Agent Westcliffe was a cautious man.

'Cap!' His face looked startled in the mirror. 'What –'

'Open up!' Kennedy didn't like the light, the target he presented. 'Quickly!'

The light died, the door opened, and he stepped into a dim corridor. Bolts jarred behind him and Westcliffe stood facing his visitor. He was plump, his body rounded beneath the fabric of an embroidered robe, leather slippers on his naked feet. His hair was long, plaited with silver cords, dyed a brilliant azure. His hands were gemmed, the nails long and stained with purple. He looked exactly what he purported to be, a rich merchant dealing in precious spices. Only the gun in his hand was out of character.

He said, 'I didn't expect you so soon, Cap. I was just getting ready for bed.'

'Are you alone?'

'I've two servants – both long asleep.'

'You sure of that?'

'I'm sure.' Westcliffe looked grim. 'They stay in their own part of the house behind locked doors. I don't want them to know more than they have to.' His tone lightened as he smiled and lifted his hand. 'Hell, Cap, it's good to see you!'

Kennedy looked at the gun.

'Sorry.' Westcliffe slipped it into a pocket of his robe, held out his empty hand. His fingers, like the rest of him, were plump, but muscle lurked beneath the fatness. 'You certainly wasted no time.'

'You said it was urgent,' reminded Kennedy. 'Or so I was told. I caught the first ship available, got a berth as second engineer, and landed only a short while ago. Where can we talk?'

Westcliffe led the way into an inner room, a large place lined with books, a desk occupying the center, soft carpets on the floor, tables bearing vases, statues, objects of value. He crossed to where a decanter stood beside goblets of engraved crystal, poured wine, and handed one of the brimming glasses to his visitor. His eyes widened as he noticed what had been invisible in the dimness of the passage, the jagged rip on the shirt, the ugly stains.

'Trouble, Cap?'

'Some men tried to jump me on the way from the field.' Kennedy touched one of the stains and saw the redness of blood. From the man whose head he had crushed, he guessed, or the other who had held the gun. He threw it on the desk as he tasted the wine.

'Armed men?' Westcliffe examined the weapon. Breaking open the magazine, he looked at the load. Slim pointed cylinders of grayish substance. Self-propelled missiles which vented the sum total of their energy on impact. 'Cheap,' he commented. 'The barrel worn and the action slow. You could hit someone close but it's useless for long-range work. I'll give you a better one before you leave.'

Kennedy sipped his wine. It was pale green and held the scent of lawns, the taste of mint. 'Will I need it?'

'On Tulgol it's crazy to go unarmed.' Westcliffe was firm. 'Carry a gun and let them see you have one. Use it if you have to. Damn it, Cap, you know that.'

Kennedy knew it, but a second engineer didn't carry arms and he had wanted to stay in character. A transient drifting around the lawless worlds. A man who had arrived at Tulgol by accident and who would take his time getting to know the local ways.

He said, thoughtfully, 'The men who attacked me wanted to capture, not kill. At least that was what one of them told me. He could have been telling the truth. I didn't give them time to find out.' He sipped a little more of his wine. 'On the other hand, they could have been watching. They could have seen me land and followed me to kill. In which case you could have a leak.'

'No.'

'How can you be certain? No spies on Tulgol?'

'Too many, but I took all precautions and no one could have known you were coming. Damn it, Cap, even I didn't know. If I had, I would have sent men to the field.'

Which was exactly why Kennedy had traveled the way he had. Agents, even those as experienced as Westcliffe, sometimes overlooked the obvious. Kennedy watched the man as he helped himself to more wine. Safe, snug, and wealthy in relation to this world. An ambitious man might forget his prime loyalty and be tempted to use his position for his own gain. It had happened before and could easily happen again. Men, no matter how dedicated they might be at the beginning of their service, could be corrupted and subverted by the very environment in which they worked.

Such men did not last long.

Was Westcliffe one of them? Kennedy doubted it, though it was always possible. They had worked together before and knew of the steel resolve which resided beneath the façade of gross conviviality. But the attack in the alleys had still to be explained.

'It happens,' said Westcliffe grimly, as Kennedy probed the

19

subject. 'Too damned often. Men killed, maimed, left in the gutter. Mostly the reason is one of greed. A careless spacehand, a quick attack, and he is left stripped and robbed. If lucky, that's all he loses.' Again he refilled his goblet, setting down his glass as he caught Kennedy's eye. 'Habit,' he explained. 'In the circles in which I have to operate drinking is a social custom. More deals are made over a bottle than in any other way. The trick is to get the other man tight while you stay sober.' He patted his rotund stomach. 'I've one hell of a capacity, though I say it myself. The fat helps, of course, that and practice.'

'Nice for the vintners,' said Kennedy dryly.

'They get by.'

'And you?'

'I work for Terra,' said Westcliffe flatly. 'Just as you do, Cap. And I never forget it.'

Kennedy finished his wine. Setting down the goblet, he said, 'I was questioning one of the men who had attacked me when he was shot by someone lurking in the darkness. I fired back and maybe hurt him. That isn't important. What is, is the reason why the man should have been killed at all. Someone wanted to shut his mouth. Why?'

Westcliffe shrugged. 'I don't know.'

'You can guess. Would a normal night-gang be set up that way?'

'No.'

'That's what I thought. So it couldn't have been a normal robbery. It's always possible that someone may have recognized me as I left the field, but if they had just wanted to kill me, why the attack? I could have been shot down from a dozen places. One man with a gun could have taken care of it.' Kennedy glanced at the weapon lying on the desk. 'That gun. So we can eliminate attempted assassination. The attack doesn't fit in with normal robbery. So either they were a group of junkheads after a thrill or something else.' He paused, then added, 'And junkheads wouldn't have had a man lying in wait to take care of a talker. So what's left?'

The question was rhetorical; he knew the answer before Westcliffe breathed the word.

'Slavery.'

'On Tulgol?'

'On Tulgol and other worlds.' Westcliffe sat at his desk, his face suddenly old, the eyes seeming to have sunken back in the contours of his face. 'Too many men have vanished, Cap, on here and other planets. Men are always disappearing, that I know. They move on, they die, they drop out of sight sometimes to reappear, more often never to be seen again. But there have been too many of them recently, and always of the same type. Young men, mostly, fit, strong, spacehands, laborers, servants, even. They just vanish. And there is something else.'

He opened a drawer of the desk and dipped in his hand. When it reappeared, it held a mass of living fire.

'Look!' He spread a half dozen gems on the surface of the desk.

Kennedy leaned forward, inhaling, his eyes narrowing as he studied the stones. They were round, glittering with facets, the surface catching and reflecting the light in a multitude of rainbows. He picked one up, turned it against the light, fingers deft as they felt the texture. Picking up the discarded gun, he rapped the muzzle against the stone. A thin, high, crystalline sound sang through the air.

'Chombite?'

'Yes,' said Westcliffe.

Kennedy struck the gem again, listening to the sound, knowing that he held a small fortune between the fingers of one hand. As a gem it was beautiful, but it was far more than a bauble to be worn by a rich woman or as an advertisement of his wealth by a bloated merchant. The crystalline structure was capable of holding an infinite amount of stored knowledge. The one he held could replace the conventional memory banks of a computer, could act as the repository and relay mechanism of the most sophisticated equipment.

'They're coming on the market,' said Westcliffe grimly. 'Offered on free sale. I've obtained all I could within the limits of my apparent wealth, more would arouse suspicion, but there's no end to the damn things.'

Kennedy said quietly, 'Synthetic?'

'Natural.' Westcliffe stirred the little heap of gems. 'I've tested them a dozen ways and there's no doubt. They've been expertly cut and polished and matched for size.' He picked up the stones and let them fall from one hand to the other. Shimmers of light reflected from his eyes, the smooth roundness of his cheeks. 'Chombite, Cap. Trouble.'

More than trouble, thought Kennedy grimly. A woman would mortgage her soul to own a matched pair, a man sell his labor for a decade in order to wear one in a ring, but such avarice was harmless. The trouble would come from repressed worlds, power-hungry rulers, cultures dedicated to the overthrow of accepted law. Chombite would give them the instruments they lacked, the spaceships with computerized systems, the relay stations, the monitoring devices which would open the doors to achievement. And more.

A scrap of chombite in the guiding system of an atomic missile would steer it across the vastness of space to land on any designated target. The power of the gems would feed the engines which drove the ships at faster-than-light velocities. Power. Real power. The force which would make worlds obey the whim of a ruler insane with paranoia. Obey or be destroyed.

Replacing the gem, Kennedy said, 'The source?'

'Unknown.' Westcliffe spread his hands. 'I've tried, Cap. I've had men asking and paid for rumors. Bribery, blackmail, you name it and I've tried it. No success. If anyone knows the source, they aren't talking. Terra has checked on all known sources of supply and these stones didn't come from any of them. You know how security is in those places: you couldn't get out with a grain of dust, let alone stones of this size. And I've got a half dozen of them. Others could have more. Every rich merchant wants one for his wife or daughter. For what those would bring here, in this city, I could retire and buy a farm on some Inner World.' He paused, then added softly, 'God knows what they would bring on a world such as Zad. Twice as much, perhaps? Three times? Who can tell?'

'On Zad you would get promises, lies, the stones taken and instruments of torture given you in their place. You would tell where more could be found or you would die in screaming agony.' Kennedy's eyes were hard, direct. 'You want to try it?'

Westcliffe shook his head. 'Not me, but others? That's what I'm afraid of, Cap. What Terra is afraid of. Once a lunatic like the Prince of Zad gets a hint of what's available, all hell will break loose. He'll sell his world for ships and men and missiles, then go on a rampage across his sector of the galaxy. And he's just one. I can think of a dozen more, the petty rulers of small worlds with ideas. way above their capability. Give them chombite and you give them the power to run riot. We both know what will happen then.'

Delicate alliances broken. Blood and death spread across the stars. Suspicion and distrust created beneath the threat of war.

An ape was relatively harmless when armed only with a club. Give it a rifle and it was dangerous. Give it an atomic bomb and all men would have cause for fear. A fear which could only be resolved in the destruction of the ape.

And . . . if the ape had friends?

More destruction.

Perhaps destruction without end.

A destruction which could even reach to Earth itself.

Kennedy thought of the parks and recreational places, the teeming cities, the heart and center of the Terran sphere which held a part of the galaxy in civilized restraint. On the Inner Worlds men needed to carry no arms. A woman was safe. Children could grow in comfort and security. The long, hard climb from blood-soaked mud was finally over and new frontiers had replaced the old. But Earth was not an old world dreaming in the sun. Peace had been won at too high a price for that, and the lesson too hard to forget.

Eternal vigilance is the price of liberty.

And Earth intended to remain free.

Which was why agents like Westcliffe were resident on worlds scattered throughout the galaxy, and other agents, Free Acting Terran Envoys like Kennedy, did what they could not.

He said, 'Missing men and chombite from an unknown source. It adds up, Westcliffe. Is there more?'

'Two ships reported missing from the Tormas Sector.' Westcliffe produced charts, listings, a heap of graphs from within his desk. 'The area is one of small, backward planets, traditional cultures, hereditary rule, that kind of thing. There are some mines and a scatter of industries. Free traders make a living serving the various cultures, shipping supplies, acting as agents for specialized machinery, the usual thing. Two vessels at least have disappeared. They left and didn't arrive at their destinations.' He shrugged. 'By itself that isn't too unusual. The ships out there usually operate on a shoestring and most of them are little better than scrap. However, the ones which vanished both carried mining equipment.'

'Piracy?'

'Not unusual out in the Tormas. A valuable cargo is an invitation for trouble. But who would want to steal mining equipment?'

'A lot of people,' said Kennedy. 'If they knew where to sell it.'

'That's what I thought.' Westcliffe glowered at his papers. 'So I put a man to search out what he could find. Arden Hensack. You know him?'

Kennedy shook his head.

'He was my assistant. Sent out for training and possible replacement. A nice young man, with ambition. I haven't got a son, Cap, and – ' Westcliffe broke off, shaking his head. 'Well, never mind that now. He vanished.'

'Snatched?'

'I hope so. I don't like the alternative. He could have asked one question too many, perhaps, or let something slip. If so, he must be dead by now. That's when I asked for help. This thing's too big for me to handle, Cap.'

And it wasn't his job to try. Westcliffe was an eye and ear and helping hand. He had already done too much by using his assistant, risking his own established cover for the sake of curiosity perhaps. Kennedy hoped it was no more than that. Good agents were hard to find and Westcliffe was one of the best. But a good agent knew when to act and when to wait.

'Chombite,' said Westcliffe, reading Kennedy's thoughts. 'I had to try, Cap.'

'So you tried,' said Kennedy. 'And lost a man. Let's hope that's all you lost.'

'It was enough. More than enough.'

'Maybe.'

'You think he talked? Told them about you?' Westcliffe shook his head. 'No. He couldn't. Not talk, I mean. With the right persuasion anyone can be made to talk. But he doesn't know you. He couldn't have described you. There could be no connection between those who attacked you and what I sent him to find.'

'You're wrong,' said Kennedy harshly. 'And you know it. Stop trying to defend Arden Hensack. I'm not blaming him, so there's no need. But someone tried to snatch me and it was a well-handled operation with a killer standing by in case of need. That means organization. There's a market somewhere for cheap labor and there's someone who is supplying it. Point one. Ships containing mining equipment have been stolen. Point two. Chombite is a gem which has to be mined and it's finding its way on the market from an unknown source. Point three. Do I have to add it up?'

'I've already done it,' said Westcliffe bitterly. 'Why do you think I called for help? It's obvious when you put the pieces together. Slaves. Mining equipment. Chombite. A fortune for someone and a hell of a lot of trouble for plenty of others. It's got to be stopped, Cap, and we both know it.'

Stopped before it could get out of hand. If it wasn't already past redemption. Kennedy studied the charts, lists, and graphs as Westcliffe helped himself to wine. The ship disappearances were relatively recent. The mysterious vanishings of men a little later. The gems?

'They've been around for a while,' admitted Westcliffe. 'There was talk, hints, suggestions of a good investment. A couple of people I know mentioned them to me and I bought as soon as it was possible. Once I saw what they were I began digging.'

Kennedy leaned back, his eyes thoughtful. Deliberately he imagined himself to be in the position of someone who had stumbled on a new source of chombite. What would he do? How would he act?

An honest man would sell the find to recognized authority. A less honest man, or one with more imagination, would do what? Work it himself for the sake of high profits? Mining was expensive and a single man could hardly back an honest operation. So what then? Get a few of the gems, use them to obtain money to be used as bribes. Cash in order to hire technicians to mine more gems to get more cash to expand the workings? It made sense and fitted the pattern.

He looked again at the charts and graphs. If men were being snatched on Tulgol and other nearby worlds, then the source must be close. His finger traced lines, rested on an area of space. The missing ships had been near that area. The men could have been taken there. Technicians could only be found on planets with a high enough technology to support them. This world, perhaps? That one? He checked the listings; Westcliffe had done his preliminary work well. Like a computer Kennedy's mind traced lines of probability, jumped intuitively to logical developments of events.

This area, then. But space was vast; the area held a dozen worlds.

He said, 'If I wanted to hire someone on Tulgol to find me workers, cash down and no questions asked, who would be the best man to see?'

'Macau Grimbach,' said Westcliffe without hesitation. 'He's

shrewd, clever, and as dangerous as a man can get. He doesn't come cheap, though.'

'Chombite isn't cheap. If I had gems to give him?'

'Then he'd be your man.' Westcliffe looked at Kennedy as he rose from behind the desk. 'Do you think he's behind all this, Cap?'

'I don't know,' said Kennedy grimly. 'But I have to find out.'

'You, Cap? Alone?'

'Alone.' There was no time to wait for others. 'Now tell me where Grimbach is to be found.'

CHAPTER FOUR

It was past midnight when he left the house and no one seeing the figure stumbling down the alley would have recognized it for the trim, hard man who had landed a short while ago. Stained leathers blurred the outline of shoulders and waist, his face was grimed, his hair a mess. A gun rode on his hip, the butt worn, matching the greasy belt and holster. He looked vague, quarrelsome, and more than a little drunk. A drifter, ship-jumper, a man low on cash and lower on patience.

A part Kennedy could play to perfection.

He stumbled from the alleys and stood blinking in the garish light of the joy sector. A ten times larger-than-life girl simpered and extended a brimming glass, the luminous contents vanishing as she raised it to parted lips. Another, eternally dancing, beckoned to a door wreathed with garlands. A third, smaller, toyed with dice, chips falling in a glittering rain from fingers and hands. Pipes and drums stirred the air, muffling the shouts, laughter, and yells which throbbed and echoed all around. A place of noise, brightness, pounding confusion.

Kennedy thrust his way through the crowded sidewalk, shoulders hunched, eyes glowering as they searched the flaring signs. Macau Grimbach, so Westcliffe had told him, owned a place known as Wilma's and, if on Tulgol, would be there. It was a large place, the roof a fantasy of spires and turrets from which hung glowing balloons puffed into strange and wanton shapes. The door was an arch flanked with giant flambeaux, the open portal guarded by a pair of Phen dressed in ceremonial costume.

They were eight feet tall, monstrous in plates and scales of armor, pikes gripped in taloned hands. One stooped, staring at Kennedy from beneath the pointed visor, nose-tendrils twitching as he examined the potential customer.

His companion hissed, 'Permitted?'

'There is doubt. Something – '

'Get away from me!' snarled Kennedy. The Phen were rudimentary telepaths, employed to keep out potential troublemakers. 'Away, I said,' he repeated as the grotesque creatures hesitated. 'Move or I'll rip the whiskers from your snout. Can't a man get himself a drink and a little fun without having freaks give him nightmares?'

Glowering, he strode past the guards and into the building.

It was what he had seen a thousand times before. Tables, drinks, men and women hysterical with drug-induced euphoria or sitting, blank-eyed, watching the bounding balls, the various devices at which they hoped to gain a fortune.

An attendant, neat in gray and maroon, sidled up to him, eyes hard as he studied the strained leathers, the pistol hanging low.

'One warning, mister. Start anything and we'll finish it. Maybe you'd do better to go somewhere else.'

'I was recommended,' said Kennedy. 'Get to Tulgol, they said. Get to Wilma's. Grimbach will look after you. Is he in?'

'Who?'

'Grimbach. Macau Grimbach. Your boss.'

'This place is owned by Wilma,' snapped the attendant. 'She doesn't like trouble. Have your drink, make your play, but remember what I told you. One step out of line and we'll crush you.' His foot slapped down on the floor. 'Like a bug.'

Kennedy said, harshly, 'Is that a threat?'

'You're damn right it's a threat, but if it makes you feel better call it a promise.' The attendant sucked in his breath. 'Just watch it. Whatever you start we'll finish.'

He moved away and Kennedy crossed to a table where colored balls bobbed in a cloud of luminescent gas. After ten seconds of agitation one ball was expelled and those who had backed it were paid according to the odds. Yellow paid highest, then blue, green, orange, and red. Red paid even; a gift to the house because only one ball out of three was red.

He moved on, halting at a dice game, his mind calculating the odds. Again the house was favored but he backed, playing with skill, winning small but regular amounts, and then, as if impatient, he played half his winnings on an impossible combination.

He lost as he had known he would, and moved on to yet another game.

A waiter passed with a tray of drinks. Kennedy snatched one, swallowed it, grabbed another. The waiter frowned and, beyond him, Kennedy could see the attendant watching. Satisfied, he returned to the game.

An hour, he thought. Time enough for his presence to be noticed, for his actions to be marked. The Phen had been uneasy, the attendant half inclined to throw him out; only the certainy of trouble had prevented him. Now he would reinforce his assumed character, that of a tough man careless of danger, skilled, ruthless, and impatient. If Macau Grimbach was around, he would know of Kennedy's actions. If not then, maybe, he would learn.

He gambled, swore as he lost, gambled again. A youth backed, treading on his foot, and he slapped the boy's face, snarling. Leaning forward, he grabbed the dice, rolled them, watched as they fell.

'Loaded!' He leaned over the layout and snatched at the dealer. 'The damn things are loaded! I want my money back!'

'Now really, sir!' The dealer was white, his eyes wide with terror. 'I assure you that – '

'Trouble?' The attendant was back, his voice a feral purr.

'It's this man, sir!' The dealer tore himself from Kennedy's hand. 'He seems to think that the dice are loaded. He wants his money back.'

'Give it to him.' The attendant smiled at the ring of watching faces. 'There are no crooked tables at Wilma's. If this man thinks that he has been robbed, then return what he has lost. Will that satisfy you, sir?'

Kennedy was sullen. 'I should have won. I bet and, had the tables been honest, I would have got back three times what I put down.'

'The stake only,' said the attendant. The fingers of his right

28

hand closed over Kennedy's left bicep. They dug like hooks of steel. 'Give it to him.' He stood, bland as the money was handed over. 'Are you perfectly satisfied, sir? You are? I thought that you would be. And now, if I may escort you to the door?'

It was smoothly done. Those watching would see only a semi-drunken drifter being soothed and escorted from the premises. They would never guess that outside, where others would be waiting, the troublemaker would be beaten, robbed, stripped, and maybe left lying dead. Or, perhaps, thought Kennedy grimly, they had other plans for him. Maybe he too would join the ranks of those who had vanished. For a moment he was tempted to ride along, to follow the route others must have taken, but the risk was too great. And, as yet, he had no proof that Macau Grimbach was behind the kidnappings.

As they neared the wide door he said, 'Take your hand off me, mister.'

'Shut your mouth, scum!'

'I want to see Grimbach.'

'You'll kiss the dirt,' promised the attendant. 'All you're going to see is stars.'

Kennedy turned, his right hand, the fingers stiffened, stabbing like a spear at the other's midriff. The attendant doubled, gasping, rising as the hand lifted to chop at the underside of his jaw. Supporting his limp weight, Kennedy looked around. To one side of the arched portal a door stood behind a velvet hanging. He reached it, tore it open, passed to the stairs inside as a voice lifted from the room behind.

Dropping the unconscious man, Kennedy raced up the stairs, found a passage flanked with doors, ran down it as feet padded up the stairs behind him.

'Gene? Hell, Malepo, he's out cold!'

'Never mind him.' The voice was deeper, almost a growl. 'Get that character before he can reach the others.'

'But . . . Gene?'

'Damn you, man, do as I say!'

Two of them at least and there would be more. Kennedy reached the end of the passage, found more stairs, raced up them, gun in hand, eyes alert for signs of danger. A door stood ajar to his right. He halted, pressed it open, looked at a chamber hung with tapestries and filled with the scent of perfume. A woman sat before a mirror gilding her hair.

She was big, not fat but large-boned with a smooth expanse

of silken flesh running in sweeping curves from neck to ankle. She wore a gown of some shimmering material which caught the light and haloed her with nacreous luminescence. Her face was round, the eyes deep-set and startlingly blue; her lips were pursed in a rosebud and from the lobe of each ear hung a pendant of sparkling gems.

She said quietly, looking in the mirror, 'Who are you?'

'A stranger,' said Kennedy. 'Sam Dulain. A friend told me to look up Macau Grimbach if ever I was on Tulgol. Are you his woman?'

'I am Wilma.'

'His woman?'

'His business associate. Do you intend to kill me?'

Kennedy glanced down at the gun in his hand. He thrust it back into its holster, shaking his head.

'I'm sorry,' he said. 'I had a little trouble down below. It seems that Grimbach isn't easy to reach. I think I made a few enemies on the way up. The gun was for insurance.'

'I see.' She was incredibly calm. Setting down the spray which she had been using on her hair, she said, 'Either you are intensely brave or incredibly foolish. A brave man I could use; a foolish one would be better dead. Why do you want to see Macau?'

'I want a job.'

'Doing what?'

He had no opportunity to answer. Behind him the door crashed open and two men boiled into the room. They were armed, their pistols rising as they saw Kennedy. He saw the flash of light on the barrels, the eyes, narrowed with intent; then he was falling, leaping forward as he fell, his stiffened hands chopping at knees and ankles.

He felt bone yield, heard a cry like a scream, then weight thudded across his shoulders and something slammed viciously above one ear. He felt the impact, saw the gleam of metal, and shook his head to clear the blood which ran into his eye. The pistol barrel had torn the skin of his temple, half stunning him with the force of the blow.

He rolled, kicked, jerked up a knee and then was on his feet, one hand lifting to catch the wrist, to turn the threatening gun away from his face. For a moment he faced a big man with a prominent jaw, twisting to avoid the knee which thrust at his groin, jerking back his head to save his eyes from clawing fingers. Then his left hand rose, stabbing, the tips of the fingers driving deep into the throat, impacting the nerves beneath the skin.

Paralyzed, the man fell.

'Nice.' Wilma stood at the far end of the room. The gold of her hair, the smooth curves beneath the lustrous gown, the gems which glittered from her ears gave her a regal, imperious appearance. An effect which was heightened by the gun in her hand. It was small, the barrel chased with gold, the butt encrusted with gems. The bore was aimed at his heart.

'I must warn you,' she said quietly. 'I am an excellent shot. If you move or reach for your gun, I will kill you.' She glanced at the men lying on the floor. 'Neat,' she commented. 'I like to see a good fight. They should never have attacked at the same time. One should have stayed back while the other moved in. But I suppose they wanted to impress me. Fools. Sometimes I think I am surrounded by fools. A pity you had to join their number.'

'Did I?' Kennedy shrugged, his eyes watchful. It was barely possible that he could manage to escape her first shot. No matter how concentrated a person was, how intent, any action took time. She would see him move, decide to fire, send a mental message to close her finger on the trigger. A fraction of a second, perhaps, but there would have to be a delay. If he moved fast enough, kept moving in random directions, he could, possibly, escape her fire.

'Don't try it,' she said. 'No matter what you're thinking, don't try it. This is set on automatic. Once I press the trigger the gun will spray your end of the room with missiles. The magazine holds a dozen. Twelve shots all in a restricted area. You're a gambler – what odds would you give against your getting hurt?'

'None.'

'I'm glad you said that. I called you a fool – I'm pleased you're not trying to prove me right.'

Kennedy said, 'If I can't see Macau Grimbach, could I have a drink?'

'Are you sold on that stuff?'

'I can take it,' he said, 'or I can leave it alone. Mostly I have to leave it alone.' He had caught the contempt in her voice. 'I'm a spacer. That's when I'm not a rock miner. I've done other things too. You want someone taken care of? Just give me his name and the price. He'll never bother you again. You want some boys to work downstairs? How about giving me a section? No cheating, no complaints, nothing to worry about. And I won't act like Gene. He was stupid. Maybe he's learned by now just how stupid. Ask him to tell you – when he can talk.'

On the floor the man with the prominent jaw stirred, groaning.

'My neck!' He sat up, rubbing his throat.

'Forget your neck.' Wilma didn't look at him. 'See what's wrong with Tony.'

'His knee's broken,' reported Malepo after a moment. 'His jaw too, by the look of it.' He rose, scowling. 'Shall I take care of this character, Wilma?'

'Could you?'

'Just give me the chance.' He sucked in his breath. 'He caught me unawares before. Tony got in the way. The next time –'

'He'll probably kill you,' she snapped, interrupting. 'You're out of your class. Try it again and you'll deserve all he gives you. Tell Sincet I want him.'

'Leave you alone?' Malepo thrust out his jaw. 'Now listen, Wilma –'

'Do as I say!' She didn't raise her voice but there was no need – the tone was enough. 'Get Sincet.' As the man left she said to Kennedy, 'You want work, right?'

He nodded.

'And all that performance downstairs was just to get an audience with Grimbach?'

'Yes.' He glanced around the chamber. 'Can I see him?'

'You'll see him, but not here. You're a spacer, you say?'

'That's right. I can handle an engine and navigate if I have to'.

She said, rapidly, 'You're on a course to an inner world and the drive blows. You've emergency power, no more. The sun is getting close. What do you do?'

'Use what power we have to drive in a tangent toward the sun. Its gravitational field will give us sufficient velocity to break clear in an elliptical orbit.' He added, quietly, 'Did you expect me to say that I'd use the power to fight the gravity well?'

'Some would.'

'Some probably have done it,' he agreed. 'But we can never

really know. Those who tried it are dead now. No emergency power can withstand the direct gravitational pull of a sun. You have something in mind for me?'

Wilma looked at the gun in her hand and then, as if by impulse, threw it on the dressing table. It landed with a clatter of pots and vials, a puff of powder rising as it struck against her cosmetics.

'I've a job for you,' she admitted. 'Or I can give you the chance of one. It isn't easy, but the pay will be good. It'll take a hard stomach and plenty of nerve. If you want to quit, turn around and walk out now. I'll give you that much because I think you've earned it. But it's the last chance you'll get. Once you take the job, you're in it to the end.'

'What is it?'

'Macau will tell you that. If he decides to take you, that is. Interested?'

He had come too far to back out now and, if this was the only way to see Grimbach, then it had to be taken.

'Yes,' said Kennedy. 'I'm interested.'

She relaxed, smiling. 'Good. I'm glad you said that. Good men are hard to find. Sincet! Take him to the ship.'

He was standing in the doorway, waiting, a gun in his hand. A soft-footed, soft-voiced creature. A mutated man with peaked ears and fur on his head and face. He put away the gun, bowing as he said, 'As you wish, my lady.' And then, to Kennedy, 'Now, my friend, let us move!'

CHAPTER FIVE

The ship rested in thick shadows at the edge of the field. A long, slender, wicked-looking craft more at home in the void than resting on the impacted dirt. The main hatch was open, men lounging in the flood of light. They could have been taken for a normal crew eager to snatch a few last breaths of planetary air before embarkation, but Kennedy knew better. This was no normal crew and there were far too many for a ship the size of the *Quell*.

An under-officer, broken-nosed, scowling, glared at Kennedy. 'Who's this?'

'A new one,' Sincet purred. 'Take him to Macau, Karn. If he passes, you'll be riding with him, so treat him gentle.'

There was an undercurrent in the purring voice which Kennedy caught but could not understand. A subtle message, perhaps, or the sharing of a private joke. He filed it away in his mind as he followed Karn through the hatch and into the ship. It was well-kept, the plates clean, the fittings polished, even the floor unusually free of the scuffs and scars common to any vessel which had seen long service. Karn halted at a door, tapped, opened it at a summons from within.

'The new one,' he said, and pushed Kennedy inside.

So he had been expected. Kennedy glanced around as the door closed behind him. The cabin was neat, the furnishings luxurious. Two men stood at the chart table, one obviously the captain. He was tall, broad, his face scarred with pits, the corner of one eye puckered from an old injury. He wore the usual leathers, shoulders and elbows polished from long suit-contact.

The other man had to be Macau Grimbach.

He was small, elegant, ruffs of lace at wrist and throat. His clothing shone with brilliance, metal insets catching and reflecting the light, gems glinting in bursts of shimmering glory, threads which seemed to twist and move with a life of their own. He looked a dandy, a fop, but his eyes were those of a snake. Cold, brooding, veiled with secret calculation.

He said, 'You are dirty. You need a bath.'

Kennedy bridled. 'Now listen –'

'You listen!' The voice was thin, the cutting lash of a whip. 'For some reason you impressed my associate and I have agreed to give you employment. But get one thing clear. On this ship Captain Wei is the boss. If he says "jump", then you jump. Is that understood?'

'I've ridden ships before,' said Kennedy sullenly. 'I don't have to be told.'

Wei said, sharply, 'What was your last vessel?'

'The *Athone*.' Kennedy had been briefed by Westcliffe and mentioned a vessel which had left two days ago. 'I had a little trouble, so I didn't sign on.' He paused, then added, 'Sir.'

'Position?'

'Cargo handler, sir. It was all that was going. But I can handle an engine and –'

'Yes, yes,' snapped Macau impatiently. 'On this voyage such skills will not be needed. Work hard, work well, be loyal and you will be well-paid. Captain?'

The owner was subtle. He could give the order but no captain liked to be given orders when on his ship and never before a crewman. Wei pretended to consider it.

'We don't really need another crewman,' he said. 'But, well, I'll take him along.'

'Thank you, Captain. Wilma, I am certain, will be pleased at your decision.' Macau touched a scrap of fabric to his lips and the scent of perfume filled the cabin. 'And now, if we could finish our discussion?'

Outside Karn was waiting. As he led Kennedy toward a cabin he said, 'What's your name? Sam Dulain? Right, Sam. I'm Karn. You take orders from me. Remember that and we'll get along.'

Kennedy said, 'When do we leave?'

'Soon.'

'Where to?'

He felt the slap, the hard impact of the palm against his cheek, and crouched, snarling. He could have avoided the blow, could have caught the arm and sent the officer to the deck screaming with pain, but he was supposed to be a drifter short on temper but desperate for a job. So he glowered, fingers twitching at his belt, the low-slung gun.

'That's your first lesson,' snapped Karn. 'I don't want to have to repeat it. If I do, I'll break your jaw. No questions. Remember that. You don't ask questions and you don't get curious. Just do as you're told. Get nosy and you'll wind up in space without a suit.' He pointed to a door. 'Get in there. Find yourself a bunk and wait.'

The cabin contained the typical furnishings of crew quarters. Bunks, a washbasin, a shower, a few chairs around a table. Men sat in the chairs gambling with a greasy pack of cards. Others lay on the bunks. The air smelled stale, overused and badly adjusted as to humidity.

As Kennedy entered, the play stopped and he was the focus for all eyes. One of the men said, 'Name?'

Kennedy gave his alias.

'You want to join in, Sam?'

'What with? I'm broke.'

'Aren't we all?' Another man gave a short laugh. 'We play on credit. If you want to join in, you start with a hundred. Karn will sign a chit.'

'Sure,' said another. 'He'll sign a chit for a hundred and give you eighty. A nice, friendly type, is Karn.' His eyes narrowed as he spotted the red patch on Kennedy's cheek. 'I see you've learned just how friendly he can be.'

Kennedy scowled. Among such men his best defense was to be sullen, taciturn. Finding an empty bunk, he stretched, thinking.

The ship was obviously overcrewed. The men around all bore the same stamp: drifters, hardcases eager to earn some easy money. But if the vessel was about to leave, they should have been at their stations, not sitting, idle, playing cards, or asleep as most of them were. So there had to be others, the regular crew perhaps – in which case, why were these men here at all?

Time, he thought, would tell.

He blinked, conscious of a sudden fatigue. At the table a man yawned, stretched, yawned again.

'Hell,' he complained. 'I'm tired.'

'Me too,' said another. 'Joe?'

Joe was already asleep, lying sprawled across the table, his breath fluttering the cards. As Kennedy watched another joined him, then two more. The air held a harsh, acrid tang.

It could only be gas. Kennedy inflated his lungs and held his breath. Rising, he crossed to the door and tested the panel. It was locked. Thoughtfully he studied the cabin. If Macau was as clever as his reputation implied, there would be scanning devices monitoring the area. Even now an officer, Wei himself, perhaps, could be watching. If Kennedy remained conscious, he would immediately be under suspicion.

He staggered, caught hold of the edge of the table to save himself, then weaved back to his bunk. He flopped, turned, and deliberately exhaled. Breathing deep he tasted the gas, the acrid tang, and felt his senses begin to reel. Two more breaths and he slipped into oblivion.

He woke to stare at Karn's broken nose.

36

'Up!' snapped the officer. 'Get on your feet. You've had your rest, now it's time to work. Move!'

Kennedy blinked. 'What's going on?'

'Up, damn you!'

Kennedy rolled from the bunk, dodging the thrust of the club which the officer carried. His mouth felt dry and his throat ached with the need of water. His belt and holstered gun had vanished and he noticed that all the others had been disarmed.

'My gun?'

'You'll get it back later.' Karn's voice rose to a bull roar. 'Listen, all of you. There's food and water waiting. You'll eat and then you'll work. Now move! Get on your feet! Come alive!'

The food was a rich, thick stew heavy with protein and laced with vitamins. With it came a thin, tart wine which held a medicinal taint. Eating, Kennedy wondered how long they had been kept unconscious. Hours certainly, days probably, maybe even a week or more. Time enough for the ship to have left Tulgol and to have reached a destination. He leaned back and rested his ear against the metal of the hull. There was no sound of engines or the slightest trace of vibration. If the ship had moved, then it had come to rest.

Beside him a man scooped up the last of his stew.

'That was good.' He sighed. 'What happens now?'

Karn didn't keep them waiting long. He stood before the door, the club prominent in his hand, his broken face harsh in the glow of the lights.

'I'll give it to you straight,' he snapped. 'You wanted work and now you've got it. If you don't like it, that's just too bad. Outside there's a lot of stuff to be loaded aboard. You're going to do it. If anyone wants to complain, I'm the man he should see. If anyone wants to argue, the same.' The club lifted in the big hand, threatening, vicious. 'Just do as I tell you and everything will be fine. You'll get high pay and maybe the chance of more work later. Argue and you'll get a smashed skull.'

'Hell, Karn,' called a man. 'Who's arguing?'

'Just lead us to it,' said another.

Another, cheerful because of the wine, said loudly, 'Who do we fight, Karn? Who do we kill?'

There was no need to fight and there was no intention to kill.

Kennedy stood outside the hatch and looked at the devastation beyond. Once it had been a small community of huts,

37

sheds, dormitories, grading houses, and chutes. The fabrications remained but where there should have been controlled activity there was nothing but silence. The mine which should have been working was still.

A tower was a smoking ruin. A squat building which had once held ports and weapons had been blown apart. The ground was rutted, torn by missiles. In the pale light of an azure sun the limp bodies of men lay sprawled among wilted flowers and crushed plants. Others lay close to the ship, still more at the entrance to the mine working. Ringing the area suited figures stood with power-packs on their backs, the squat barrels of hetdyne projectors in their gloved hands.

Not all the limp figures were dead. As Kennedy watched, one of them moved, turning, rising to its knees, one hand reaching for the rifle which lay to one side. A suited figure caught the movement and lifted the muzzle of his weapon. As the man tried to bring the rifle to bear the hetdyne projector emitted its spiteful wail. Paralyzed, the man slumped, his central nervous system thrown into chaos by the heterodyning waves.

'Get him,' snapped Karn to one of the others. 'Put him into hold seven. Move!' He turned as the man raced away. 'You others, follow me into the mine. There's equipment we need. Hurry! We haven't got all day!'

A raid, thought Kennedy as he followed the officer. The *Quell* had dropped from the skies at about dawn. Without warning the ship had blasted the defensive installations of the mine, drenching the area with gas, following the anesthetic with the suited men and their projectors which would stun but not kill. Some miners had obviously managed to fight back only to be ruthlessly cut down by guns from the ship. The others, helpless, could only yield.

And, while it had happened, he and the others had been asleep.

Asleep, knocked out, kept in storage until they would be needed. Labor to load the vessel with the fruits of the raid. Porters, not trusted, with weapons, now needed to lift and hump. Brainless muscle to be smashed down and destroyed if they should object.

At his side a man said, 'I don't get it. What's the good of secondhand mining equipment? Who could want it?'

'I don't know,' said Kennedy.

'Men too. Why?'

The wine had dulled his faculties, that or he had no imagination. To Kennedy, struggling with the massive bulk of a machine, the answer was plain. Machines to use on a mine and men to work the machines. A neat, cheap, and easy way of getting the things essential to work rock and stone. Neat, cheap, and easy, if you didn't count the cost in human lives and wanton destruction.

This had been a nice, calm, normal operation. Men delving for the sake of what they could find. The jungle pressing close and bringing with it the scent of flowers. Danger must have seemed very far away. The product must have had a relatively small value or their defenses would have been more than token installations. And then the *Quell*, falling quietly from space, the sudden blast of its guns, the savage attack.

The gas, the suited figures, the sharpshooters in the vessel. And now the scavengers to collect the loot.

The men and machines which violence had won.

And he was a part of it.

A slaver!

Kennedy kept his face low so as to hide the burning hatred in his eyes. There was nothing he could do as yet; any offensive act would result in immediate death, and it was too late to save the mine. But now he had the proof that Macau Grimbach was more than casually involved in the hated trade of slavery. His ship and his men had been used in the attack. One day, perhaps, he would pay for it.

'Hurry!' Karn stood, bawling. 'Move there! Get that stuff aboard. Hurry!'

A file of men staggered by, dazed, their bodies still twitching from the effects of the hetdyne projectors. Like animals they were prodded into the bowels of the *Quell*. An old man stumbled and almost fell. Karn lifted his club, the weighted end whistling through the air to land with a soggy crunch of splintered bone.

'Old,' he snapped. 'And too damn weak. He wouldn't be worth his keep.'

All day the work continued, men sweating as they hauled machines from the mine to the ship, dismantling when they had to, using brute strength when it could be avoided.

At dusk a siren wailed over the clearing and a general rush started for the open port.

Karn stood by it, counting. He grunted as Kennedy jumped

39

through the opening, waited for two others, then gave the signal. The port sealed, a bell chimed, and the ship lurched as it rose, engines whining as they responded to the surge of power.

Karn sighed. 'I couldn't have wanted it better,' he said. 'A nice, neat, fast job and no unexpected trouble. You did well, Sam. I had my eye on you. You got stuck in and kept moving. Not like some of the others. They want cash, but they don't want to work for it. You tied in well. Keep it up and you might earn yourself a bonus.'

'Thanks,' said Kennedy dryly. Congratulations from a murdering slaver was something he could do without. 'What happens now?'

'Remember what I said about asking questions?'

'I remember, Karn. But if you hit me again, I'll kill you. That isn't a threat. It's a promise.'

Karn glared at him, eyes narrowing in the broken face. 'You mean it,' he said softly. 'By God, you mean it. You couldn't do it, but I guess you'd die trying. Hell, Sam, why spoil it? A shut mouth is worth money in this game.'

'If it lasts,' said Kennedy flatly. 'I wasn't asking questions, Karn. Not that kind of question. But I'm interested in what's going to happen to me. I don't like being gassed.'

'You know?'

'I worked on a zoological expedition once. We used to gas the beasts and I got to recognize the signs. So you've your own reasons and I'm not arguing, but I don't like it. Not with the cargo we're carrying. Those miners could break out and, if they did, we wouldn't stand a chance. They're tough and they outnumber us and they won't be gentle. We'd be gutted or thrown out without a suit. That's what I was talking about.'

'They're locked in,' said Karn. 'And we keep them gassed most of the time. But you're right; we do need guards and you can be one of them. Shift and shift about. When you're on watch, you work on the ship.' He dropped a heavy hand on Kennedy's shoulder. 'We'll get along,' he promised. 'Just trust me and you'll have nothing to worry about.'

Kennedy said, 'You've done this before, Karn?'

'More questions, Sam?'

'I just want to feel safe.' Kennedy paused, then added, 'And I'd like to get rich. Anything wrong in that?'

'Not a damn thing, Sam,' boomed Karn. 'Not a single damn thing. Play along and that's just what you'll be. Rich.' His hand fell again, heavier than before. 'Now get along and eat while you've got the chance. Eat and sleep for a while and then get down to work. Move!'

CHAPTER SIX

There was no chance to help the prisoners. The work consisted of cleaning the vessel, polishing, rubbing, doing empty, routine tasks which kept him close to the holds in which the miners were secured. He was given no arms, only a weighted club, and always there were others within earshot. Karn trusted no one. The captain was seen only once a day during routine inspection, and if Macau Grimbach was aboard he kept himself completely out of sight.

Time passed. Kennedy chafed with impatience, yet knew there was nothing he could do. Dutifully he performed his routine tasks, watching, studying the layout of the vessel. Even that was frustrating; the regular crew prevented access to the engine room, the communications shack, the control room, and other vital parts of the vessel. They were curt, contemptuous, barely masking their dislike of the extra hands who, as far as Kennedy could see, served no real purpose now that the vessel was loaded with slaves and equipment.

And then came the gas.

Kennedy smelled it as it came. An acrid odor hanging on the air, almost indistinguishable from the other smells, the taints carried by air overused and stale. The product of recycling mechanisms overstrained by the burden imposed by the miners, the extra crew. Quickly he inhaled as he had done once before, chancing the vapor taken into his lungs against the main bulk yet to come. An ordinary man, with training, could hold his breath for about three minutes. Kennedy could hold his far longer, using mental disciplines to slow his metabolism and to negate the discomfort. He lay motionless, throwing himself into a half-aware state in which he was dully conscious of the deepening breaths of the others, the small sounds they made as they fell into oblivion.

The journey had taken too long. The air was growing bad, the water stale, and the food must be running low. Unless Captain Wei was more than a fool the voyage must soon be over. The gas was proof of that. Elementary precaution dictated that secrecy be preserved and that the extra hands, like the prisoners, were better rendered unconscious so as to be incapable of harm.

Lying supine on his bunk, Kennedy waited.

Lights began to dazzle his vision and an iron band constrict about his chest. He concentrated on mental divertissements, using the Ghengach system of disorientation aided by the Clume Discipline. The lights vanished, the band eased, and, floating in a self-induced hypnotic state, he became detached from his present situation. Continued to an extreme the disciplines would have enabled him to be buried alive, there to remain dormant for days, as had the old fakirs of ancient Earth.

There was no need of that. After several minutes he cautiously sniffed and smelled nothing but familiar odors. The acrid taint had gone. Releasing his breath he inhaled, waited, then reoxygenated his blood with deep breaths of air. Still he did not move, giving the observer, if anyone was watching, time to be convinced the gas had taken full effect. After fifteen minutes, he rose and tested the door. It was locked as before. Stooping, he examined the catch. It was a simple tumbler operated from the other side, the mechanism sealed from within.

Kennedy smiled.

He opened his leathers and tore free one of the magnetic fastenings. Holding it to the lock, he listened, moving the small magnet in a complicated pattern, catching the tumbler with its invisible field and lifting it from its catch. The door yielded a little beneath his hand and he rose, opening it a crack to stare into the passage outside.

He froze at the sound of footsteps.

'All secure, Karn?'

'As you ordered, Captain. A double dose to keep them quiet as we determine their future.' The officer's voice held a grim amusement. 'There's a couple who might be of use, if you should so decide. Joe Mulgrave and Sam Dulain. I've been watching them. They could be suitable for promotion.'

'Maybe.' Wei didn't sound too sure. 'I don't like taking a risk, especially when there's no need. We can always find more drifters.'

'As you decide, Captain.'

'It would be best to let them all go. Make a clean sweep while we're at it. The less there are to talk, the safer we shall be. I don't want some spacehand in the future trying to avenge a brother or a friend.'

'A friend?' Karn made a contemptuous sound. 'Scum like that have no friends.'

'Maybe not, but they drink, and a drunken man can talk and maybe someone will hear. It's best to take no chances. Keep them all under and we'll pass over the whole batch.' Wei chuckled. 'A fine crop, eh, Karn?'

'The best yet, Captain.'

'Our contact should be pleased. Well, we'll be making contact soon. The usual procedure, Karn. See to it.'

'Aye, aye, Captain.'

The footsteps died away, ending in the sound of a closing door. Kennedy released his breath, his face grim as he digested what he had heard. It came as no surprise: the extra hands engaged with promises of high pay and easy reward were expendable. More slaves to add to the others, their numbers swelling those of the miners. He felt no distress at what he had learned; they were as much to blame and, in a sense, it was poetic justice.

Almost he could have enjoyed it – if he had not been one of their number.

The door opened and he stepped out into the passage. Aft it led to the holds where the miners were held, and for a moment he hesitated. If he could reach them, revive them in some way, they would make a force which could easily take over the ship. But he remembered the holds were fastened with locks and chains with men on constant guard and probably automatic mechanisms to give the alarm. The other way then. Forward to the control room, the radio shack, and navigation tables. If he could determine the position of the *Quell* and radio the information to Westcliffe, others, if necessary, could take over.

A crewman stepped before him as he reached the end of the passage.

The man had been lounging, standing routine guard, discounting any possibility of danger. He stared, his eyes and mouth opening, the gun in his hand slowly rising.

'What do you want?'

Kennedy smiled. 'Message for the captain.'

'From where? Hey, you aren't – '

He doubled as Kennedy's hand slashed at his throat, the stiffened edge impacting the nerves and bringing swift unconsciousness. A door stood behind him giving on to a small cubicle filled with emergency gear. Bottles of oxygen, patches, a lightweight suit, containers of bubbles to be released in case of hull-penetration. Kennedy heaved the unconscious man into the room and slammed the door. The gun in his hand, Kennedy raced down the passage and into a room packed with electronic equipment. A man turned as he entered, froze as the muzzle of the gun touched his temple.

'Our position,' snapped Kennedy. 'Give it.'

'I can't.' The radio operator sweated as he tried to look at his questioner's face. 'I don't know it.'

'Try again.' Kennedy's lips thinned as he twisted the muzzle. 'Our position!'

'I tell you I don't know it!' Fear shrilled the operator's voice. He shrank back in his chair, trying to escape the pain of the pistol barrel grinding at his temple. 'I've just come on duty, but even then it makes no difference. The captain doesn't tell anyone where we are. I just sit here and wait for a message.' He gulped as a lamp flashed on the panel. 'This must be it.'

'Take it.' Kennedy tensed as the man reached for switches. 'Full vidéo and make no sign that I've got this gun at your back. Say a wrong word and I'll blast your spine.'

He stood, apparently relaxed as the screen filled with light and color. A face sharpened, became that of a scaled monster with a flaring crest and wide jaws savagely fanged.

'Operation calling *Quell*. Answer.'

'*Quell* here,' said the radio operator. 'Code?'

'X1567GH4. Respond.'

'S2139TK2.'

The slotted, goat-like eyes lifted a little, stared directly at Kennedy. The crest flushed a little, a delicate pink suffusing to a pale orange.

'Repeat.'

'S2139TK2.'

Something wrong. Kennedy could sense it and he felt a tightening of his stomach. The radio operator could have given the wrong code or could have left something out. It had been

44

impossible to guard against such a thing and, though he could kill the man, the damage had been done.

On the screen the creature sucked at his fangs and said, 'Understood. A good trip?'

'Fine.'

'That is gratifying to hear. Inform your superior that contact is to be as arranged. You will do it immediately.'

Kennedy felt the radio operator tense. He said, flatly, 'That will not be necessary. I am the new captain of this vessel. Give present coordinates for necessary adjustment of instrumentation.'

It was a wild hope and he wasn't disappointed when the image vanished to be replaced by a drifting cloud of motes. And all was not lost. The creature had been a resident of Obrac, a member of the Ghazen and, if nothing else, it narrowed his search. The Ghazen owned few ships and had fewer captains. It shouldn't be impossible to find the one who had spoken.

To the radio operator he said, 'I warned you. You told him something was wrong.'

'No! I swear it!'

'Don't lie to me! I told you what would happen if you didn't play along.' Kennedy lifted the gun. 'You damned slaver! Think of those men killed back at the mine! The others you are helping into a life of hell!'

'For God's sake!' The man was desperate. 'Don't kill me! I'll do anything! Anything!'

'The coordinates?'

'I don't know them. The captain handles the piloting and navigating alone.' He swallowed as he looked up at Kennedy's face, the hard determination of the eyes. 'We arrange a rendezvous and take on a pilot. Please, mister! I don't know where we are. Don't kill me!'

Kennedy dropped his left hand to the man's shoulder, gripped, dragged the cringing figure upright. Coldly he said, 'We're going to the control room. You will walk ahead and remember I've got this gun at your back. Try anything foolish and I'll fire.'

The ship jerked as they left the compartment, a harsh grating singing through the hull and causing the bulkheads to quiver. It came again and Kennedy staggered, almost losing his balance. From the control room came Wei's angry snarl.

'The fool! What's the matter with the man? Is he blind?'

'I don't understand it.' Karn's bull roar was subdued, afraid. 'That's twice he's hit us. If I didn't know better, I'd think he was trying to ram us.'

'If he does it again, I'll blast the fool.' The captain was seething with rage. 'Get to the radio, Karn. Make contact. Ask that pilot what the hell he thinks he's doing.'

Kennedy knew he had only seconds before discovery. His one chance was to reach the control room and hold those inside at gunpoint while he determined their position. Once found it could be transmitted and, afterward, with luck he might be able to take over the vessel. He wasn't given the chance.

Karn's bulk loomed ahead. He snarled as he saw the radio operator.

'What the devil are you doing here? Get back to your station.'

'I – '

'You!' Karn had seen Kennedy. He could not see the gun. 'How did you get out? What's going on?' Without waiting for an answer, he lunged forward down the passage, his club lifted.

Kennedy thrust the radio operator into his path.

They met with a thud of flesh, Karn's roar rising above the other man's scream as the club lashed at his head. Like an eel, Kennedy darted past the interwound figures, springing into the control room, lifting the gun as Wei turned to face him from where he stood at the controls.

'Don't move!' snapped Kennedy. 'Touch anything and I'll kill you!'

The captain was alone. Kennedy stepped aside as Karn came from the passage, halting as he saw the gun. The radio operator, stunned, emitted a low moaning as he lay in the passage.

Wei said, 'Have you gone insane? Do you really think you can get away with this?'

'I can try.' Kennedy glanced beyond the captain to where screens showed a vista of stars. Against them the sleek bulk of a small ship hung uncomfortably near. As he watched, it began to drift closer, tiny points of lambent flame jetting from the steering tubes.

'What do you want?' Wei's voice was controlled, almost calm, belying the fury which smoldered in his eyes. 'Money? Promotion? Put down that gun and you can have both. Main-

46

tain this charade and acid will dissolve every inch of your skin. Karn!'

'Don't move!' Kennedy's finger tightened on the trigger as the officer stepped forward, his broken face ugly with hate. 'Better yet, lie down. Flat on your face with your arms extended over your head. Do it.'

'You're an intelligent man,' said Wei as Karn obeyed. 'You know that one man with a gun cannot hope to take over a vessel. You could kill me, perhaps. You might even be able to kill Karn and others. But what then?' He glanced at the screens, the ship edging close. 'And you have underestimated the situation.'

His voice rose to a shout. 'Zagout!'

Abruptly Kennedy was fighting for his life.

CHAPTER SEVEN

It had dropped from above, a shimmering thing of wire-like tendrils interspersed with hooked nodes and suckered pads. A curtain of vibrant life built like a net, an expanse of lace. It dropped over his head, his arms, tendrils tightening about his wrists and fingers, jerking, pulling, holding them close. He managed to fire once, the missile exploding in a gout of fire against the deck, then the weapon had been wrenched from his hand and he felt the blood pound in his skull as cramping pressures closed over head, neck, and ribs.

Muffled, blinded, unable to breathe, he poured strength into his arms and hands, the fingers hooked, tearing at the constricting tendrils, ripping away delicate-seeming fragments which held the stubbornness of tensile alloy. Then he fell, rolling, to end hard against the bulkhead, helpless in a living cocoon.

Through a pattern of lace he saw Wei's face as the captain stooped over him.

'An ingenious device, is it not? A life-form from Yalathen which I have trained to be of service. It lies dormant on the

47

ceiling until commanded to act. A small precaution against the unexpected. At this moment it waits for a second command. Once I give it, it will crush you to pulp.' Then he added, viciously, 'But not yet. First we have more pressing matters to attend to. Once they are taken care of, your death can begin. It will not be an easy one. The constriction will be slow. You will feel every second of it and each second will seem like an hour. Think of it while you wait.'

Behind the captain Karn said, 'This ship is getting too damn close for comfort. It looks as if they are going to hit us again.'

'As a warning, naturally.' Wei straightened. 'Get that fool of an operator. Establish contact and tell our friends that everything is under control. Exchange to take place immediately.'

'And this one?' Karn loomed over the helpless figure. Deliberately he slammed the toe of his boot against Kennedy's shin.

'Later. Now do as I order.'

Kennedy heard the diminishing thud of boots. The pain from his shin was a white-hot fire, the embrace of the creature a prison which held him fast from head to knees. Cautiously he tried to move and felt the wreathing tendrils close even tighter. It was all he could do to breathe.

From the bulkhead he caught various sounds: the impact of metal, the hiss of air, the scrape of boots as the exchange was made. Mentally he visualized what was happening. The ships lying close, suited figures moving from one to the other as the pilot came aboard the *Quell* from the other craft. A cunning system evolved, perhaps, in the brain of Macau Grimbach.

Men employed to act as porters, those same men to later join the slaves they had helped to obtain. A secret rendezvous. A strange pilot who alone knew their ultimate destination. He would take over the *Quell*, running it from the control room until it was time to land. And then, once the cargo had been discharged, the same procedure would take place in reverse.

Clumsy, expensive, but efficient. No one aboard the *Quell* would know where the slaves were to be used, the source of the precious chombite.

He caught the scent of perfume and rolled his eyes, looking at a familiar shape. Grimbach was resplendent in gaudy colors, gems winking from his hand, and he sniffed at his scrap of fabric. Beside him stood the monstrous creature he had seen on the screen. It dwarfed the figure of the man, the crest riding high, tinged with a pale blue.

'This is the one,' it boomed. 'The one I saw in the radio shack. I guessed something was wrong.'

'You were right, my lord,' said Grimbach. 'I must congratulate you on your quick thinking.'

'I ordered the ships to be impacted. I knew that your men would heed the warning.'

'As they did. Correct, Captain?'

'He's safe,' said Wei. 'You recognize him, sir?'

'Of course. The man Wilma asked me to employ. She was obviously correct in her suspicions. He isn't what he seems to be.' Grimbach stooped low, his face inches from Kennedy's eyes. 'Tell me, friend: just who and what are you?'

Kennedy fought for breath.

'Sam Dulain,' he said painfully. 'I grew suspicious and wanted to play it safe. I guess things got out of control.'

'Indeed they did,' said Grimbach blandly. 'And most unfortunately for yourself. As they did for that other one. A nice lad. I was sorry to see him go. He could have been a friend, of course. Arden Hensack. Did you know him?'

Kennedy tried to shake his head. 'No.'

'I think that you are lying.'

From where he stood behind the others Karn growled, 'Let me work on him. He'll talk. I swear it.'

'And say what?' Grimbach touched the scented fabric to his nostrils. 'That our activities have aroused curiosity and interest and someone wants to know more about them? We anticipated that, so it comes as no surprise. And does it matter? Our precautions are thorough and we work in free space. Even so, it is a pity that someone as courageous as this man must die. But, there it is. The luck of the game, you might say. The rule of life. The strong exist at the expense of the weak. And you, my friend, at this moment, are very weak.'

Grimbach turned, fluttering his scented scrap of material. He looked bored.

'I think we may as well bring this episode to a conclusion, Captain. If you will give the command?'

Kennedy strained at his bonds. The living tissue eased a little and he concentrated, inflating his chest, summoning the power of the Clume Disciplines to channel his trained strength.

A tendril parted with a snap, another ripped apart oozing

ichor, a third stretched to allow his hand to rise, to grip a node, to rip at the yielding tissue. He felt the thing shudder, the burn of hooks as they dug into his flesh, the sear of liquids against his naked skin. The shimmering hues flared, faded, flared again to turn dull.

Wei stepped forward. He said in a harsh tone of command: 'Zagout – '

His words choked off as a scaled hand clamped over his mouth. Elgha Zupreniz, his crest burning with the blue of pleasure, watched the struggle with slotted eyes.

'Let them fight,' he boomed. 'Struggle is the destiny of man. Even you soft creatures have to fight in order to live.'

Kennedy heard the words through a haze. The command to crush had not been given, but the alien creature had not waited for it. The rule of survival had overridden its training and now it exerted all its power to destroy the man within its tendrils. The hooks tore, the thin, steel-like strands bit deep, deeper as one pulled against the other. Kennedy fought against them, his chest a flame of agony as he fought to breathe, to feed his system with essential oxygen. He concentrated on the nodes which, he guessed, must hold the rudimentary brain. The web of ganglions which gave the thing direction and purpose.

One shredded under his fingers, the nails digging into the rubbery surface. Another pulped beneath a shoulder as he slammed his back against the bulkhead. A third he reached with his mouth, strong white teeth tearing it apart. The taste was vile, but he mastered the desire to vomit, continuing the attack, gaining a little slack here, a trifle more freedom of movement elsewhere. Hooks ripped at his scalp, filling his eyes with blood. He blinked them clear, throwing back his shoulders, jerking his head, never for one second letting up on the fury of his attack.

The thing hissed, a high-pitched, ear-aching scream of released internal pressures. The shimmering hues flared with an eye-bright kaleidoscope of reds and greens, blues and sultry yellows and for a moment Kennedy was wreathed in a pattern of glory.

And then it died. The hues faded. The tendrils grew quiescent. What had been a glowing curtain of brilliant color became a ragged net of somber brown.

'He killed it,' said Wei blankly. He had jerked himself free of

50

the constricting paw. 'He tore it apart with his bare hands. But that's impossible. It can't be done.'

Elgha Zupreniz rumbled his satisfaction.

'He did it. Never have I seen anything like it before. Had I been told I should have doubted the teller. Truly my friends, I must thank you for a most stimulating entertainment.'

Wei scowled, looking at Kennedy, still wrapped in the tendrils of the dead creature. The thing had been hard to obtain, harder still to train, and now it was gone. It had served him well on more than one occasion and now he felt a sense of loss. Not because of the creature, but because in dying it had robbed him of a certain measure of protection.'

And Kennedy was still alive.

He said, 'Karn. Take care of it.'

Karn grinned. He stepped forward, club lifted, an ugly light in his eyes. This he was going to enjoy. Kennedy had lied to him, caused him to misjudge character, and make himself appear a fool before the captain. He had even recommended the man for promotion. So, first the shins, then the knees, and after that the groin. Then the tip of the club in the face, the eyes. He had done it all before.

Kennedy watched as he came. The eyes in the broken face betrayed the sadistic pleasure Karn was feeling. And he remembered the old man at the mine. The smash of the club which had crushed his head. The casual blow as if Karn had killed a troublesome fly.

He tensed, adjusting his muscles, resting his weight on his upper back, his shoulders. His feet drew in a little as if in fearful anticipation of the club.

'Afraid, you scum?' Karn sucked in his breath. 'See how you like this!'

Kennedy felt the deck beneath his elbows. The tendrils still held him close, dead though they were. He couldn't dodge or use his hands and arms. Instead, he turned his whole body into an instrument of destruction.

As Karn stooped to deliver the first vicious blow, Kennedy exploded into action.

His legs lifted, his back arched, and he lashed out both feet with all the force of back, thighs, and shoulders. The heels of his boots caught Karn beneath the chin, smashed into his throat, threw the big man backward to slam against the edge of the control panel. He toppled, vomiting blood, dead before he hit the deck.

As he fell Kennedy kicked out again, using his body like a spring, rising with acrobatic agility to land on his feet.

'Hold!' Elgha Zupreniz knocked down the gun Wei had produced. 'This man must not be killed like a beast.'

Macau Grimbach said, 'Do it, Captain.'

'No!' The Ghazenian glared from one to the other, his crest tinged with orange. He, the Lord of Sergan, to be defied by such weak, troublesome things! Alone he could take them both and crush them to death in his talons. 'I insist!'

Grimbach sighed, reaching for his scented fabric. Always it was troublesome to deal with other life-forms and always he found their customs to be beyond his understanding. Caution dictated that the man be killed immediately before he could do more harm. And yet was his life worth a quarrel which could cause the loss of immense profits?

Carefully he said, 'My lord, with respect, the man is a danger. And he is also on my ship. Therefore I have the right to decide his fate.'

'Decide as you will,' snapped Elgha Zupreniz. 'But he must not be harmed. Not by you. Such a fighter deserves a better end. And, if we are talking of spacial custom and jurisdiction, let me remind you that now that my pilot is aboard this vessel comes under my authority.' He raised a clawed hand, impatient at the discussion. 'Enough. Let the man be put aboard the other ship. And let us attend to matters of business. You have how many slaves? And equipment? Good. The Baron will attend to the details of payment when the goods have been delivered.' Grimbach bowed. 'As you order, my lord.'

'Always as I order,' growled the Ghazenian. 'Remember that.'

'Will you not be coming with us?'

'No.' The clawed hands lifted, rubbed together. 'I have other plans.'

The arena, he thought. The hot sun and the crowds and the thrilling exultation of combat. His champion set against those of others. The thrag of Dulen Yanchiga, the croat of the Fenedish clan. The beasts of which they were so proud and of which they had boasted so long.

And now he too had a champion. A man who had killed against all odds, who had survived the attack of a vicious

52

creature and who had killed what had seemed to be unkillable. A soft, helpless-seeming thing devoid of scales or armor, with hardly any fangs and no talons, but who had proved himself beyond doubt. A fitting addition to the retinue of the Lord of Sergan.

CHAPTER EIGHT

Obrac was a hot world, close, the air thick with jungle scents, the sun a blazing furnace which turned deserts into ovens, the streets of the city into a baking hell. The houses were low, fretted with ornamental arches, spires and cupolas wreathed with vine bright with blossom. From behind blank walls came the sound of running water, the tinkle of fountains, and the rill of streams. And there was music, the whine of scraped gut, the pulse of drums, the hard, sharp rattle of impacted wood.

The Ghazen, obviously, liked their comfort.

A splayed hand thrust against Kennedy's back and a harsh, guttural voice snapped a command.

'Keep moving. This is no sight-seeing tour. The quicker we get out of this heat the better.'

One of the crew of the ship to which he had been transferred. A sleek, rounded creature with an oily hide, webbed hands and feet, eyes like marbles in a hairless skull. A Liganian from the aquatic system of Coronalis. Hard, tough, ruthless. As much at home in the sea as on land. Perfect mercenaries whose greatest ambition was to buy an undersea castle there to settle and breed.

Kennedy said, 'Cut out the rough stuff. This heat's just fine.'

'For you, maybe, not me.' The Liganian scowled, a bristle of whisker to either side of the wide mouth lifting in twin tufts. 'This wasn't part of the deal,' he complained. 'Handle the ship and that was all. Take care of any trouble, but nothing else. I don't like to see the contract broken. Once it starts, where will it end? You do a little more than you're paid to do, and then get taken advantage of. I don't like it.'

'You could do something about it,' suggested Kennedy. 'Turn around, go back, take the ship, and head into space. Work for me and I'll guarantee you get twice the pay you've been offered.'

'No,' said the Liganian firmly. 'That would be unethical. Once we sign a contract, it's binding. Keep moving now.'

They reached a house taller than the rest, a twisting spiral rising from the flat roof. Inside it was cool, high ceilings arching to points, softly humming mechanisms distributing the scented air. A servant took Kennedy down to the basement where stood a ring, the appurtenances of a gymnasium. Two young Ghazenians were wrestling, claws rasping against scales, their crests burning orange. A third watched them. He was squat, his scales thick with warts, his crest torn and ragged. As one of the contenders slipped and fell he slashed his talons against the surface of a gong.

'That's enough,' he boomed. 'Get washed and oiled. Jehar, learn to watch your opponent's feet. Velat, you were slow. A quick bite in the third engage would have won you the bout. Remember this, the pair of you. You've claws, teeth and talons. Use them all and you might, just possibly, make a show in the arena.'

The old pit-master shook his head as they left the ring.

'Young,' he said. 'They think they know it all. Old as I am I could take on the pair of them and still come out on top.' He glared at Kennedy. 'So you're Elgha's new champion. Sometimes I think he's trying to make a fool out of me. Thirty years in the arena, fifteen kills, and more token claws than I can count, and he sends me a thing like you. Well, what else can an old man expect? Bed, board, and a place in his retinue. Some young fools to train and a prime seat in the arena. Catch!'

Kennedy caught the flung ball. It weighed over a hundred pounds. He threw it back to land hard against the trainer's chest.

'Neat,' he boomed. 'At least you're fast and seem to have some muscle. Is it true that, bound and helpless, you managed to kill one of your own kind?'

'Yes.'

'Have you killed often?'

'I kill when I have to,' said Kennedy flatly. 'And for no other reason.'

'Good.' The trainer threw aside the ball. 'I don't like these youngsters who lust to kill. They get careless and won't listen to advice. It's a matter of reputation, you understand. When I train a man he has to be good. His failure reflects on me.'

Kennedy said, 'Is this Elgha Zupreniz's house?'

'It is.'

'And he is the Lord of Sergan?'

'That's what he calls himself.' The trainer shrugged. 'What's in a name? Five times I was crowned King of the Arena and where has it got me? If there was any justice I would be sitting at the head of the table with first choice of wine and viands. I would have an establishment of my own with clients from all over the planet. Well, there it is. One man is hatched to power; another steps from his egg to a life of deprivation. Strip now and let me see what you can do.'

For an hour Kennedy exercised, lifting heavy weights, doing sit-ups, running, jumping, punching a heavy bag filled with sand, tuning up muscles which had grown a little slack during his confinement aboard the ship which had brought him to Obrac.

He halted at the sound of the gong. The trainer, his ragged crest a dull brown, said, 'Looking at you I think the rumors must be true. Elgha Zupreniz has gone mad. Why else should he take as his champion a creature like yourself?' His claws rested on the hard skin of Kennedy's shoulder. 'Soft,' he complained. 'Not a scale for protection. One good rip and you'd be dead. What manner of sport does he hope to provide?'

Kennedy shrugged. 'None, I hope.'

'You hope. You are afraid?'

'A man would be a fool not to be.'

Slotted eyes, dull with age, blinked as the trainer considered the reply.

'You have a right to be fearful. A croat is not the most gentle of beasts and that owned by the Fenedish is a prime specimen of its kind. Already they have won two estates and beggared three families with its aid. Rich though Elgha Zupreniz has become, he would be insane to pit you against it.' He shrugged. 'Well, time will tell.'

Kennedy said, 'Where is Sergan?'

'Somewhere.' The pit-master was weary, and impatient to

bask in the sun. 'I cannot be concerned with such matters.' He beat the gong and, as a servant answered the summons, said, 'Take this creature to the room prepared.'

It was small, containing a narrow bed and nothing else. The window was arched and glazed with colored panes. They opened as Kennedy jerked at the fastening and he looked outside. Beyond lay a vista of roofs, a great circular amphitheater, the distant pylons of the spacefield.

Thrusting his head and shoulders through the opening, Kennedy studied the building which held him prisoner.

Below, the wall fell sheer to the street eighty feet below. Four feet from the opening a narrow ledge ran to either side to meet a decorative pillar at each corner. Twisting, he looked upward and saw the crenellated ramparts of the roof some ten feet above. It would be possible, he thought, to drop from the window to the ledge, ease along it to one of the corners, there to mount the decorative pillar to the roof. From there it might be possible to make his way down to the street.

But not yet. Not until it was dark. In the glare of the sun he would be visible to any casual eye glancing in his direction.

Late in the afternoon a youth brought a jug of water and a lump of what seemed to be bread. He set down the platter and stood watching as Kennedy rose from the bed. He wore mail and harness, but carried no weapons. His crest was sharp, bright, tinged with blue.

'You're going to fight,' he said. 'In the arena. Are you going to win?'

'The arena?' Kennedy nodded toward the window, the circular amphitheater beyond. 'Is that it?'

'The finest on Obrac,' boasted the youth. 'When the pitmaster decides I am ready I will enter the lists. First I will challenge Demel Chanquil and when I have won and taken over his house I shall – '

'Wait a minute,' said Kennedy. 'Let me get this straight. You challenge a man. If you win, you take what he owns. Right?'

'If it is so decided, yes. The combat is to the death, of course.'

'And if he refuses to meet you?'

'If my claim is just, then he will lose both goods and respect.' The youth snarled as a voice shouted from outside. 'That Visier! Always he is in a hurry. One day, soon, he will have cause to regret his insolence.'

Alone, Kennedy gnawed at the food. It was thick, tasting of

meat and nuts, concentrated nourishment which needed strong teeth and jaws to master. The water was warm and faintly brackish. Replete, he lay supine on the bed, thinking.

A barbarian culture, of course, with trial by combat an integral part of the system. He had expected it, the Ghazen were a warrior race, but how could he use it to his advantage? To win fame in the arena was not only dangerous but would take too long. That was assuming he would be given the chance to meet Elgha Zupreniz on equal terms. As his declared champion he would not be given the chance. Instead, he would be set against savage creatures, fighting for wagers and spectator entertainment.

And, if he refused?

Slavery, perhaps. He would be sent to join the others but, of the two, that might be the most preferable. At least he would be able to discover just where the source of chombite was. But he might be given no choice. Elgha Zupreniz could simply have him thrown into the arena to fight or die. In such a case he would fight. He might even win. And then, having proved himself, he would be forced to fight again.

He was, Kennedy thought grimly, in a most unpleasant situation.

Night came and the city woke to strident life. The roofs became flowers of brilliance in which harnessed figures moved with splashes of shimmering color. The wealthy families of Obrac entertaining their friends; others, not so wealthy, making a show. The streets began to fill with torch-bearing runners, litters, small groups in compact formation, idlers, and loungers. The ebb and wash of life to be found in any city on any planet in the galaxy.

Like a shadow Kennedy eased himself from the window. He hung, head and arms inside, then carefully lowered himself until his boots touched the ledge. Taking a deep breath, he flattened himself with his face to the wall and began to move toward the nearest corner. The ledge was gently inclined outward, giving support only to the toes of his boots. A wrong movement, a slip, and he would plummet to the ground below.

Like a dancer he trod the ledge, hands extended to either side, his lips almost touching the stone. He felt the opening of a window to his right, gripped the edge, moved level with the panes. Inside was a small room, almost a twin to the one he had left. The youth who had brought him the food was inside. He

57

was busy polishing the blade of a sword as he sat on the bed, his face half-turned toward the window. If he should look up, then the escape attempt would be over. He did not look up and Kennedy breathed his relief as the window fell away to his left.

The decorations on the pillar were worn, smooth beneath his fingers, giving barely room for the tips of his boots. But, for a man who had climbed the bare face of ice-encrusted mountains, it presented no problem. Kennedy mounted like a cat, reached the ramparts, threw his legs over the crenellations.

Crouching against the low wall, he looked over the roof. Two guards stood before the twisting spire, chatting, their voices a low rumble. A third paced the opposite wall, a long pike in clawed hands. Two more appeared from behind the tower armed with rifles. Five men, an odd number – there should be one more at least. Kennedy found him, a dark mass against the glow of the city, standing some thirty yards to his right.

It was tempting to retrace his steps, to swarm down the pillar to the street below. He could even reach the field and perhaps arrange passage, but to do that would be to throw away the opportunity of learning what he had come to find. Kennedy thinned his lips, watching, weighing opportunity.

A door opened in the spire and a crested figure boomed, 'Quickly. Four men to attend my Lord of Sergan to the Palace. You two! You and you! Hurry!'

Kennedy relaxed. Six pairs of eyes were hard to dodge, but two should present little difficulty. He waited three minutes and then, as the remaining guards moved beyond the tower, raced like a ghost toward the door. Stairs led to the lower regions. He ran down them, freezing as he heard a familiar booming.

'Hurry! Must the Lord of Sergan be kept waiting? Where is my escort? My guards? Do I want my brothers to sneer at my late arrival? Move before I lose my patience!'

The booming faded, ended with the dull thud of a closing door. Kennedy descended another flight. The study, he thought. There, if anywhere, he would find what he was looking for. The whereabouts of Sergan, if nothing else.

It rested at the end of a short passage. A room littered with scrolls, papers, articles of price. Soft rugs muffled his boots and heavy tapestries made the place an oasis of silence. A desk stood beneath a lamp made of filigree gold set with precious gems. More gems rested on the surface in a blaze of rainbow brilliance.

Chombite. But would even a man as careless as Elgha Zupreniz have left a fortune in such plain sight?

Kennedy felt the prickling of danger and spun, eyes alert, hands lifted, stiffened for action. He saw nothing, and then a tapestry moved and a figure came into view.

It was slim, with peaked ears and fur on head and face. It wore a blouse of dull green flecked with crimson, pants of matching color, boots which shone as if cut from rubies. The gun in its hand was wide-mouthed, an instrument which could blast a cloud of killing ions at the touch of a button.

Sincet purred, 'Well, well, my friend. It seems we meet again.'

'You!' Kennedy glanced at the gems which turned the surface of the desk into a living flame. 'I might have guessed it. You and Grimbach. Are you the Baron?'

'Not I. That honor is reserved for Sina Lahari. A compatriot. I serve him as best I may.' The purring voice held satisfied amusement. 'A most profitable association, I might add. And amusing. The woman thinks I am her servant. Well, it does no harm to let her think that. There is an old proverb; you may have heard it. Take the cash and let the credit go. It is a philosophy which members of my race tend to follow.'

'Until the death,' said Kennedy tightly. 'Which, in your case, could be soon.'

'You think so?' Sincet shrugged. 'Allow me to disagree. Incidentally, if you are wondering, the passage outside is connected to various electronic devices. They warned of your coming. At this moment guards are covering the door. Should you leave, they will blast you with lasers.' His voice hardened a little. 'And now you will tell me just what you were after.'

Kennedy glanced at the gems. 'I was trapped. That lunatic intends to pit me against beasts in the arena. I thought it would be a good idea to leave. But without money I wouldn't get far. So I was looking to see what I could find.'

'A thief?' Sincet smiled. 'If so, you are a most unusual one. But it doesn't matter. You will not need the gems. Not those, at least. Instead, I will do you a favor. I will save you from the arena and I will give you the chance to lay your hands on more wealth than you have dreamed of. Amusing, is it not?'

'That depends.'

'Of course, my friend. All things are relative. But I mean what I say. Literally. I am going to take you to Sergan. To the mines. I doubt if you will live long but, while you live, you will be surrounded by wealth.' The gun lifted a little higher. 'Don't move. Don't even think of moving. Alive you are of value – dead you are nothing.' He whistled, shrilly, and as the guards came bursting into the room said, 'Take him to the ship. Tell the captain we leave within the hour.'

CHAPTER NINE

Sina Lahari spread his hands and said, flatly, 'My lord, what you ask is impossible. It cannot be done.'

'Cannot?' Elgha Zupreniz snarled with rage, his crest burning orange. 'I am the ruler of this world. There is nothing I cannot do. How dare you defy me?'

Lahari sighed, wondering not for the first time how any thinking creature could be such a fool. It had its advantages, of course, but at times his mind felt numbed, bruised by the impact of ignorance. Soon, he promised himself. Very soon now he would act and then all this aggravation would be over. But not yet. For now he had to maintain the pretense that it was Elgha Zupreniz who really ran the operation. That he was just a willing tool and a dedicated servant and friend.

'Consider the matter, my lord,' he said smoothly. 'The man you speak of is dangerous in more ways than one. You saved his life in order to use him in the arena. That is proof enough of his capability for destruction. And then?'

'Your man took him from my house. I had a match arranged, bets placed, the thing completed. He was to fight a croat. He would have killed the thing and I would have won a fortune. And now?' The Lord of Sergan lifted one clenched hand and smashed it down on the desk. Beneath the scales the plastic split like glass. 'Now I am the object of amusement. The Fenedish laugh in my face. Where is my champion, they ask. Do you know what it means on Obrac to lose by default?'

60

'I can guess,' said Lahari patiently. 'But, my lord, the man need not have won.'

'So?'

'He would have died and you would have lost just the same. Perhaps Sincet did wrong, but the thing is done and cannot be undone. What if I released him? How can you be sure that he wouldn't tell how you obtain your wealth?'

'And if he did?'

'To you, nothing,' admitted Lahari. 'But you have jealous brothers. Once they know what we are doing here, they could move in. You would be challenged and the challenges would never end. And you could be assassinated,' he added shrewdly. 'The act would be justified by our use of slaves.'

'No.' Elgha Zupreniz shook his head. 'I am the undisputed ruler of this world. All Obrac accepts that. The nobles would never dare to move against me. It is against all tradition.'

The fool was shrewder than he seemed. Lahari reminded himself not to take too much for granted. He said, 'That is true, my lord, but there are others. Let the news leak out and where will it end? Once the source of your wealth is common knowledge, enemies will arise. I know men better than you. We have taken miners, robbed ships, forced men into servitude. On most worlds that is reason enough for action to be taken. Add the wealth which lies here and an armada will move against us. Ships and men armed and thirsting for revenge. Against them we have – what? A handful of guards, some overseers, and the slaves. Your world will be overrun, you may be killed, your wealth taken. And all because of your whim regarding one man.'

Elgha Zupreniz scowled, thoughtful. At the beginning it had all seemed so easy. So very simple. Just give Lahari power and let him go ahead. The gems had arrived, things arranged, ships dropping quietly from space to discharge assorted cargoes. At the time the details hadn't mattered. He had become rich, won esteem and envy, things he had enjoyed. And there could be more. Much more. It should go on forever.

But – ?

'Perhaps you know best,' he rumbled.

'I assure you, my lord, I do.' Lahari felt a sudden relief. Already certain contacts had been made and powerful rulers interested in what he had to offer. Given just a little more time and they would move in. A colossal fortune for himself, the

Lord of Sergan eliminated, and then let the fighting start.

And it would start, of that he was certain. The tiny planetoid would become a battleground of conflicting interests. Terra itself would possibly move in with the tremendous forces at its command. Others would resist the invasion but, by that time, he would be well away, his fortune safe.

The alternative was something he didn't like to think about.

Elgha Zupreniz rose from the table and crossed to the window. His world had changed since he had first come to his inheritance and he felt a smug satisfaction as he looked at the airtight domes, the sealed buildings and processing plants where the broken rubble was crushed and the gems extracted. The hut in which he stood had replaced the earlier building. Now the air was fresh and plentiful, the walls thick, total protection against the void. Machines buried within the heart of the planetoid had taken care of the essentials, paid scientists whose greed overcame their scruples, continually monitored their products, light, heat, air, water, a stable synthetic food, even the gravitation.

Watching, it was easy to forget the slaves grubbing in the interior, the noise and dust and endless labor.

As he stared, a light began to flash on one of the buildings.

'What's that for?'

'A signal that they are about to blast.' Lahari had joined the other. 'We use digging machines, but at times a good charge can save a lot of work. There are a lot of caverns inside,' he explained. 'We've opened a few for living quarters and for the rough processing of material.' The light flashed in rapid series of pulses. 'Here it comes.'

The ground seemed to heave against their feet. It settled, heaved again, then finally came to rest. At a point far ahead the rock bulged, splintering beneath the somber light of the dying sun.

Elgha Zupreniz pointed toward it.

'Is that usual?'

'No.' Lahari frowned. 'The blast must have caught an unknown fissure. Either someone made a mistake or the rock must have been unexpectedly brittle.' He turned, crossed the room toward a communicator, and pressed a button. 'Control here. Report on blast.' He listened. 'Are you certain? But how can that be possible? Get up here at once.'

He pressed another button.

'Emergency. Send a team to seal the upper surface disturbed by the recent blast. Hurry.'

From the window the Ghazenian saw suited men pour from one of the buildings. They dragged a raft behind them, its anti-gravity unit lifting it from the ground as though it were a balloon. It held a great tank of instant-setting plastic which the suited figures sprayed on the ground with long nozzles.

At his side Lahari said, 'A precaution, only. There could be small cracks which the internal air pressure would open wide. In that case we could lose a lot of air and many workers.'

'The engineers were careless.'

'No. I've checked. It seems there was a cavity where none should have been. I've asked Te Buit to come and explain.'

The engineer was a small man with a pointed skull and the scarred cheeks common to the professional classes of his society. He carried a rolled chart which he opened on the table. His voice was high, thin, almost a whistle.

'The area was thoroughly checked two days ago when blasting was considered. A lower cavern was blocked by a wall of stone and we decided to shatter it, so as to open new tunnels. The charges were set, the area cleared, the wall shattered. The blast should have been contained to the immediate vicinity.'

Elgha Zupreniz growled, 'It wasn't.'

'That is unfortunately true, my lord.' Te Buit bowed to the Ghazenian.

'You were careless.'

'No, my lord. As I said, the area was thoroughly checked two days ago. We used sonar scan and the entire site was solid rock from the working to the surface. If it had not been solid, I would never have permitted explosives to be used. Not when the surface is exposed to the vacuum with the risk of cracking and air-loss. My professional skill – '

'You talk too much,' snapped Lahari. 'I'm not interested in excuses and neither is the Lord of Sergan. Do I have to remind you of the penalty of failure?'

'I refuse to be intimidated. My contract – '

'Stipulates that you come under the jurisdiction of this planetoid. That you abide by its rules and customs. That you agree to accpt its laws. And its laws are those which my Lord Zupreniz cares to make. If you have been careless, you will suffer for it.'

Te Buit stiffened, anger pursing the thin lips.

63

'I resent the implication of professional misconduct. Look!' He gestured at the unrolled chart. 'The sonar record as taken two days ago. As you can see, the area is solid.'

Lahari scowled at the chart. 'Your conclusions?'

'Three. The sonar could have been at fault. The charge could have been far stronger than it should have been. An unexpected and therefore unanticipated composition of rock.' The engineer shrugged. 'The sonar is not at fault. It is inconceivable that the charge could have been so much greater than intended. And the likelihood of a pocket of rock totally at variance with surrounding matter is extremely remote.'

'So it didn't happen. Is that what you are saying?'

'No, Baron,' snapped Te Buit. 'I am not. I am saying that it shouldn't have happened, but it did. As yet we do not know why. I am having the area investigated, but these things take time. I – '

He broke off as a man entered the room. He had the same pointed head and scarred cheeks as the engineer and carried a roll of graph paper. He nodded to Sina Lahari, bowed to the Ghazenian, then looked at his chief.

'We did a quick scan of the region in question, sir. There is something rather unusual. I guessed that you would be eager to learn of the results of the investigation and so brought the instrument readings to you at once.'

'What is it?' rumbled Elgha Zupreniz. He felt uneasy, at a loss when confronted with these proud technicians.

'An oddity, my lord. It explains why the blast had such an unexpected effect. Sir?'

He knew his place. A junior did not act without the permission of his senior. Te Buit took the roll of graph paper, opened it, frowned at what he saw.

'There can be no mistake?'

'None. We are running a check, but there can be no doubt.'

'No doubt about what?' Sina Lahari snarled his impatience. 'We are not playing games. I want to know what you have found and so does my lord. Explain!'

Patiently Te Buit said, 'Look at the original recording, Baron. The one taken two days ago. As you can see, the area is solid.' His finger tapped the paper to illustrate the point. 'And now look at this.' The finger moved to the roll of graph paper. 'You see?'

Elgha Zupreniz glared at the paper. 'See what?'

'An alteration in density, my lord. Incredible though it seems something happened between making the original check and the firing of the blast. A large cavern was opened above the immediate area.' His finger traced a pattern over the recording. 'A small bore seems to lead from it, though this could be a natural fault. The cavern is filled now, naturally, but the accumulated material and density of structure leaves no doubt as to what must have happened. The blast, designed to shatter a limited area of rock, broke through into the cavern and the effects reached the surface with results we have seen.'

Sina Lahari said, thoughtfully, 'So you know what caused the excessive blast. A cavern suddenly appearing where one wasn't before. Now tell me how such a thing could happen.'

Te Buit hesitated. 'It is impossible at this stage to be certain.'

'Make a guess.'

'One reason could be that the material was not homogenous. That the cavern was formed by the collapse of some unstable compound. A bed of frozen gas, perhaps, which thawed and was absorbed by the surrounding stone.'

'Wouldn't your original recording have shown that?'

'Normally, yes, but there is always the faint chance that the material could have reflected the sonar waves in exactly the same way as it would have done had it been rock.'

'You don't believe that,' said Lahari. 'What is the alternative?'

'That the rock was removed during the time between the original recording and the time of the blast. That, somehow, a cavern was formed where no cavern should have been.'

'The workers,' said Lahari quickly. 'They must have tunneled upward. They could have found a narrow fault and hoped to reach the interior of the buildings. You'd better make a thorough check of the area from both the surface and the lower workings. If they try it again and hit vacuum the entire operation will be ruined.'

Slowly Te Buit rolled up his papers. 'I don't think that can –'

'You're not paid to think,' snapped Lahari. 'You are paid to work. Now get on with it.'

The engineer stiffened. 'I wish to give formal notice of termination of contract. I will accept the penalty clause. You will arrange transportation for me and my assistants on the first available vessel.'

Sina Lahari sucked in his breath. The men were needed for

the safe operation of the mine. Later they could be disposed of but, for now, it was politic to keep them happy.

He said, 'I spoke harshly and I apologize. Both my lord and myself are concerned about the operation of the mine. Please overlook my discourtesy. If you wish to leave, I cannot stop you – but remember, the penalty clause is high. If you should stay, I can promise you a fat bonus.'

Mollified, Te Buit said, 'Well, in that case –'

'You will stay? Thank you.' Sina Lahari ushered them to the door. When he rejoined Elgha Zupreniz, he was scowling. 'Those professionals. Touchy as all hell, but we need them, for now at least.'

'To check on the workings?'

'Yes.'

'You should keep a closer watch on the slaves,' complained the Ghazenian. 'They could have hit surface and broken out. They would have died in the vacuum, true, but what would we have done for more labor?'

Lahari said, 'The workers didn't dig that cavern. They couldn't have done it. I know it and so do those engineers. At least they will when they have time to think about it. Of course, it could have been a mistake and they could be covering up their own inefficiency, but I don't think so.'

'Then?'

Lahari didn't answer. He crossed to the window and stared outside at the bleakness of the naked rock, the somber ball of the dying sun. Beneath the surface men sweated as they tore wealth from the stone. Too many men to safely handle should anything serious go wrong. And now had come the unexpected, the mysterious. It was, he thought, time to safeguard his future.

CHAPTER TEN

In the dimness a man was moaning. 'Help me! Help me! Dear God, please help me!'

It went on and on, a monotonous dirge echoed by others so that the harsh walls of the cavern whispered with a medley of sound, a combination of misery and bleak despair. From one side came the thin rill of water, adding to the sighs and groans as men twisted and turned as they sought to ease the ache and burn of overstrained muscles.

It was, thought Kennedy bleakly, a perfect example of a man-made hell.

He lay on the stone, dressed in rough pants and blouse, soft boots on his feet. His ankles were fettered, a two-foot chain between them, more chains connecting him to the men on either side. For ten hours he had been tearing at rock, using a short pick and his naked hands, stooping in a narrow tunnel, choked by dust and fragments, sweating beneath the hard eyes of sadistic guards. The gang had been fed before starting work. They had received water during the shift. They had been fed again on reaching the cavern in which they now rested: tepid soup served in edible containers. They would lie in aching misery for five hours and then be prodded back to work.

The life of a slave.

A system designed to beat a man to his knees, to break his spirit with endless labor, too little food and too little rest. Fatigue would breed apathy so that all which remained important was to work without getting hurt, to eat, to rest and find oblivion in dreams, to take things as they came. In such a condition time blurred, anger faded to be replaced by a dull, animal-like acceptance of things as they were. Until, in the end, a slave would look at his chains and forget what they implied.

Kennedy sat upright and examined his fetters. They were thick, two inches broad, riveted, and each with a double staple. The inside one held the two-foot chain which barely allowed him to hobble, the others the links connecting him to others of the gang. The chain was a quarter of an inch thick, each link welded close.

Beside him a man whispered. 'You can't wear them through. I've tried it. It's tungsten alloy and proof against anything but a chisel or torch.'

'Maybe you gave up too easily?'

'There was a time when a remark like that would have got you a busted jaw.' The thin voice sighed. 'Now I haven't the strength.'

'Or the guts?'

'Listen, mister.' The voice grew stronger, fired by the anger Kennedy had deliberately induced. 'You're new here. What have you done? Two shifts? Three? Wait until you've been here as long as I have. I'm so damned tired, I'm numb all over.'

Kennedy sneered. 'Excuses. What's your name?'

'Arden Hensack. Yours?'

Kennedy remained silent, his mind busy. Grimbach had hinted that the operator was dead, but he could have been lying, hoping for a reaction. To be chained beside him could have been a coincidence – they happened – or then again it could have been part of a deliberate plan.

He said, 'How did you get here?'

'I was looking for some friends of mine. Men jumped me in an alley. They knocked me out and I came to in a strange ship. The next thing I was here. You?'

'Much the same. Do you know where we are?'

'In a mine.'

'I know that, but where?'

Arden shrugged. 'I don't know. I passed out in the ship and woke up in chains. Since that I've seen five men die. I don't want to join them.'

'You will,' said Kennedy harshly. 'If you just sit and wait for it to happen.' Then he said, casually, 'Where did they snatch you?'

'Tulgol. I had a few drinks at Wilma's before it happened.'

'I know Wilma's. And I know Westcliffe. Do you?'

He heard the sharp intake of breath and then Arden said, cautiously, 'The spice merchant? I've heard of him. A thin guy living in the Street of Peddlers.'

'The man I'm thinking of is fat and lives in the Lane of Lanterns.'

It was a half-truth, but all he dared. If the man claiming to

68

be Arden Hensack was a plant, the less he knew about West-cliffe the better. And yet sparring would get them nowhere.

Kennedy turned, reached out, and gripped the man's throat. His face close to the pale features, he whispered, 'I'm going to play a game. I'm going to ask you a question. If you don't answer it correctly, then I'm going to kill you. Understand?'

The man gulped.

'Your number.' The code designation every agent knew by heart and which was his identification. But there was more. A code could be obtained by torture or mental probes. If the man was what he claimed to be he would know the passwords.

Arden said, 'ATAU1372.'

'And?'

''Twas brillig and the slithy toves – '

'Did ger and gamble in the wabe,' said Kennedy, deliberately misquoting.

'You've got it wrong,' whispered Arden. 'But I guess it's all right,'

Kennedy's hand relaxed. He said, 'Westcliffe must have told you he was sending for help. You should have waited for it.'

'He didn't.'

'That's right. He sent for help after you'd vanished. I'm it. Kennedy's my name.'

'Cap Kennedy?' Arden drew a deep breath. 'I've heard about you. It's a damn shame they caught you too.'

'I'm where I wanted to be,' said Kennedy flatly. 'Maybe not exactly how I would have chosen, but it can't be helped. What we have to do now is to break free, find out where we are, and get the information to where it will do the most good. Do you know anyone you can trust?'

'A few men aren't totally beaten yet.'

'Pass the word and keep up their spirits. But be careful not to arouse suspicion. When we act, we'll need all the help we can get.'

'When will that be?'

'I'll let you know.' Kennedy leaned back and closed his eyes. 'First we have to make a plan.'

He dozed, forcing himself to sleep to conserve his energy, waking to the roar of the overseer.

'Up, you scum! Up, I say!'

Bauchi was typical of his kind. A hard, savagely sadistical product of a planetary slum. Like the other guards, he carried

69

a three-foot rod of thin, flexible steel, a weapon more to be feared than a normal whip. A stun-gun was holstered at his side. It was a short-range weapon, a miniature version of a hetdyne projector. At twenty feet it could blast a man's nervous system and drop him as though he had been shot.

'Up!' The rod whined through the air and a man screamed in pain. 'Move!'

Kennedy said, 'When do we eat?'

'You hungry?' Bauchi halted before him, scowling, his head tilted as he tried to stare into the other's eyes. The rod lifted. 'Maybe you'd like a taste of this?'

'Maybe you'd like to join the gang?' Kennedy held his eyes. 'Hungry men can't work. What do you say when production falls?' His hand lifted as the rod lashed toward his face, fingers gripping, finding, and numbing vital nerves. 'The Baron wouldn't like to hear how little you care for production,' he whispered. 'Don't be a fool, man. Weren't you informed?'

Bauchi jerked at his arm. He opened his mouth, cursing; his breath stank of keel, the narcotic chewing weed which gave the first euphoria and then insanity and death.

'Check with the Baron,' whispered Kennedy. 'Sincet should have told you. I'm a plant.'

A lie, but the overseer couldn't know that. His hand trembled, and the rod lowered. 'Sincet?'

'The Baron's man. Sina Lahari works for the Ghazenian and he put me here to keep an ear open. There's a rumor of trouble. Some of that last batch.' Kennedy winked. 'You understand?'

'They didn't tell me.' Bauchi rubbed the numbness from his arm. 'They should have kept me informed,' he complained. 'All they said was to step up production.' Suspicion narrowed his bloodshot eyes. 'If you're lying I'll kill you.'

Kennedy shrugged. 'You check. Now let's have some food and go easy on that rod. Crippled men can't work.'

It was the usual tepid soup. They ate as other guards unlinked the chains from between each man, the ring of chisels merging with the spat of torches. Slow, tedious, but the safest method devised to hold unwilling men. Locks could be picked, keys stolen, but welded links needed bulky tools to force apart.

Arden whispered. 'You took one hell of a chance there, Cap.'

A risk but one which had to be taken. Kennedy would never allow drug-diseased scum to lash him into submission. And, if

70

the guard didn't check, he would have gained a measure of authority.

The meal over, they shuffled toward the workings, past humped machines which crushed the stone, lights which glowed redly in the dust, blank-faced men staggering in their chains as they came off-shift.

Pick in hand, Kennedy took his place at the head of the working, ripping free masses of stone to be passed from hand to hand down the line. He worked with a slow deliberation, apparently using every ounce of his strength but in reality conserving his energy. The men behind were not those who shared the cavern during the rest period. The overseers mixed the crews, putting the strongest at the face, the weakest to feed the machines.

There was nothing gentle in the system. It had been devised to get the best from the workers and to prevent the formation of close-knit groups.

A guard came to the head of the working. He was chewing a fresh wad of keel and his eyes were dangerous.

'You're not working hard enough.'

'I'm doing my best.' Kennedy slammed his pick at the rock. 'The point needs sharpening.'

'Use it as it is.' The overseer spat a stream of vivid blue keel juice. 'If I come up here again, you'll regret it.'

Behind Kennedy a man snarled and said, 'I'd like to get my hands on that animal. Just give me three minutes alone with him and he'd never use that rod again.'

'Talk,' said Kennedy.

'I'll prove it given the chance.'

'You and who else?'

The man blinked then, as he realized what Kennedy was getting at, and lowered his voice.

'I wouldn't be alone. A lot of the boys are willing to take a chance. It's just that we can't get together. One of them tried it and got staked out for his trouble.' He sucked in his breath. 'They got to work on him with torches. You ever smelled a man being roasted to death? Believe me, mister, it's not something you ever want to smell again.'

'I believe it. You been here long?'

'No. I was working a mine on Dephreni. Me and others on a profit-sharing basis. We was doing well and then the slaver came. They took our gear and rounded us up like cattle.' He

71

made a deep, animal-sound in his throat. 'One day I'll meet up with those who did it. When I do – ' His big hands clenched.

Kennedy said, casually, 'Did you get a look at them?'

'No. I was below and got a lungful of gas. It made things hazy. I remember a broken-nosed savage smashing in the head of an old man, but that's about all. Peegan was my friend. I'll remember who killed him.'

Karn, but he was already dead. Kennedy relaxed a little. If the man had recognized him, nothing he could say would have convinced him that he was a helpless party to the raid on the mine. But there had been others and one of them could have recognized the tall figure who had been with the others.

Water came and they drank, resting, leaning back against the stone. Kennedy sat, eyes veiled, mind busy with plans. To overcome the overseers would be relatively easy if a few acted in concert. They could obtain the weapons and head down the tunnels to the shafts which led outside. But there would be other guards armed with more potent means of destruction. Rifles, machine guns, lasers. There could be gas and, if nothing else, they could seal the mine and starve the slaves into submission.

But to delay was to invite danger. Bauchi could check or one of the miners could recognize him. The roof could fall, a drugged guard run amok, anything. He had to think of a plan.

There was Arden, the man behind him, his friends. There would be others, at least a dozen. It should be enough to make a break for the surface. They would have the element of surprise and the strength of desperation. All that really remained was to find the communication system connecting the lower levels to the surface. Capture it, dress some of the slaves as guards and –

At his side the miner said, 'What the hell's that?'

Kennedy looked at him. The man had his ear pressed tight against the stone. Following his example, he heard a dull grinding sound.

'A machine digging into a new face?'

'No.'

'A grinder, then?'

'If they had grinders, they wouldn't need us.' The miner frowned. 'I've worked in mines all my life and I know every sound every machine makes. That's like nothing I ever heard before. Listen.'

It was the same as before. A rasping, grating rumble almost as if something were chewing at the rock. As Kennedy listened, it seemed to come closer.

'I don't like it.' The miner shivered. 'It's got a weird sound. Almost as if it were alive. You see some funny things in mines. I remember once, on Xanpeft I think it was, we sank a shaft down a thousand feet and hit a bed of – ' He broke off as Kennedy lifted his hand. 'Something?'

The noise was receding. As he listened, it faded into a dull murmur, a blank silence. It was broken by the snarling voice of the guard.

'Work, you lazy scum! Dig!' His rod whined and a man shrieked, clutching at his face. 'You and you!' The rod flailed to left and right. 'You at the head there! Work before I give you a taste of this!' His hand dropped to the weapon at his belt. 'Move!'

Kennedy slammed the pick into the stone.

It sank deep, deeper than before, urged by the hatred for the guard and what he stood for exploding in a burst of energy. The handle bent as he dragged it free, struck again, ripped free a great boulder of stone. Hands rolled it down the tunnel past the scowling guard. Another and he heard the man cry out in pain.

'The rock! My foot!'

The guard snarled, stepping forward, rod lifted. Kennedy turned as a man farther down the line shouted.

'No, Fendor! No!'

The rod lashed down and Fendor turned, taking the blow on his back. The warning had probably saved his life; red with anger he had been about to attack the guard. He stooped as the thin bar struck his shoulders and Kennedy could see the clenched hands, the veins swelling in the thick neck.

He slammed home the pick, tore free a mass of stone, sent it rolling between the guard and the crouching man.

'Watch it!' he yelled.

The guard jumped back, blue juice trickling from his mouth. Drug-crazed, he was still aware of danger, the chance that he might push the men just a little too far. They would die, of course, but not before they had torn him apart.

And, if he slowed production, there would be others to face.

'Move!' snapped Kennedy, watching the man's face and guessing at his indecision. 'How can we work with you blocking the tunnel? Fendor, grab that stone!'

He had to take the miner's mind off his beating, somehow quell the man's insane anger. Now was not the time.

'Fendor!' he said again. 'Do as I say!'

The whip-crack of command had its effect. The miner shook his head, panting like a dog, then reluctantly grabbed the stone and moved it back down the line. For a moment the guard stood, watching; then, wiping the back of his hand across his mouth, he strode back down the tunnel.

'You shouldn't have stopped me,' said Fendor. 'I was ready. Another second and I'd have torn the throat from that swine.'

'And then what?' Kennedy demanded. 'We'd have been trapped in the working.' He dug his pick into the stone, relieving his own anger. 'Your chance will come,' he promised. 'But we need to get more than one when we act. Wait until the time is right and I give the word.'

He jerked at his pick, tore it free, slammed it again at the rock. The point hit, sank into the material, the haft rapping against stone. There was the sound of falling rubble, and the pick fell to show a gaping hole. And, around them, came a thin whine as air blasted through the opening.

'God!' yelled Fendor. 'You've hit vacuum!'

CHAPTER ELEVEN

For a moment no one moved. The air whined around them, carrying dust and minute fragments, tearing at hair and garments as it gusted through the opening. And then Kennedy became a blur of action.

'Rock!' he snapped. 'Get me stone, anything to block the opening.'

He gripped a lump of rubble, lifted, slammed it at the rim of the hole. Quickly he added others, working with a furious desperation, knowing that if they had penetrated to the void their lives depended on sealing the gap.

And then, abruptly, the gusting of air ceased.

'What happened?' Fendor spoke from behind. 'Did you manage to block it?'

'No.'

'What then?'

'I don't know,' said Kennedy. 'But I'm going to find out.'

He enlarged the hole and thrust head and shoulders through the opening. Beyond it was pitch-dark. He shouted and heard echoes bounce and fade to either side. He yelled again, listening, trying to determine the extent of what lay beyond the hole. A cavern, he guessed, a bubble formed perhaps when the world cooled, or made when under later stress.

Back in the tunnel, he looked at the lights. They were rad-bulbs, commonly used in underground workings. Tough globes containing a pinch of radioactive material which caused the coating within the bulb to shine with a bright fluorescence. They needed no wires, no power, and would last for years.

He said, 'We need a couple of those. Watch for the guards.'

The bulbs were held by rods driven into the stone. Kennedy slammed the tip of his pick beneath a fastening, jerked, caught the bulb as it fell. Another followed. Holding one in each hand, he returned to the opening and thrust both lights and head through the hole.

Beyond lay a smooth tunnel which ran to either side.

It was twenty feet wide, the bottom five feet below. Kennedy wriggled through the opening and dropped, dust rising from the impact of his boots. It was a finely powdered debris and he sneezed as it caught his nostrils.

From the opening Fendor said, 'You all right?'

'Yes. Come down here.'

Kennedy handed the miner one of the bulbs and examined the wall of the tunnel. It held a faint ripple, a minute corrugation as if whatever had caused it had moved in a series of tiny jerks. The tunnel curved sharply so it was impossible to see very far.

Fendor said, 'It can't open on the void or we'd have lost all our air. And no machine ever made it. There aren't any signs of chisels or laser burns. Look – the walls are almost polished.' The bulb shook a little in his hand. 'What the devil can it be?'

'A boring.'

'I can see that. But made by what?'

Kennedy said, 'Do you remember that grinding sound we heard? It came from the left and went to the right. Whatever caused this tunnel must have made that noise. Let's see if we can find out what it was.'

Holding the light high, Kennedy strode along the tunnel. The curve straightened a little and he saw a blockage. It filled the bore, a slate-gray in color, pointed, ringed with bands of glittering points. As he watched the thing began to spin, to move toward him.

'It's alive!' Fendor's voice boomed from the sides of the tunnel, went echoing to die in ghostly whispers. 'The damn thing's alive. A worm of some kind. Quick! Let's get out of here!'

'Not so fast.' Kennedy stood his ground, thinking. 'Move backward slowly,' he ordered after a moment. 'Slowly.' He added, 'And kill that light.'

The glow of the radbulb died as Fendor thrust it beneath his shirt. Kennedy held his own behind his back, the glow haloing his figure as he watched the strange creature.

The spin had increased, the glittering bands revolving as though they had been the teeth of a drill. Which, he thought, was exactly what they were. The worm was adapted to living in rock, to grind its way through it, to gain energy from what it ingested. The talc-like dust on the floor was waste matter. He stepped back as the rock-worm came closer, attracted probably by the light, the scent of food and water. It could have lain dormant for eons until woken by the sound of drills from the mine. It had moved, tearing out a large cavern, drilling toward the workings in search of a mate, of others of its own kind.

Now it advanced, quickly as it felt no opposition, heaving itself forward by muscular contraction as a worm would move through dirt.

It was reversible, thought Kennedy, able to move in either direction, forward or back as the need arose. A natural survival trait in case it met an impassable barrier.

From the hole a voice shouted, 'Fendor. The guards!'

Kennedy turned and ran down the passage, the miner at his side. Dust rose in a cloud from beneath their boots, fogging the lights and catching at nose and throat. From the opening came the sound of a scream, the whining lash of a steel rod. Kennedy reached it, dropped the radbulb and forced his way through.

He rose to stare at Bauchi's snarling face.

'You!' The overseer was shaking with anger. 'I checked. I asked who you were. You damned scum! You lied to me!'

Behind him a man whimpered, hands to his face, blood running thickly between his fingers. The rod had smashed his nose.

'You're going to pay for that,' said Bauchi thickly. 'I'm going to beat you to a pulp. No man makes a fool out of me.' He edged forward, the rod lifted, his face contorted with rage. 'Here it comes, mister. The last thing you'll ever see.'

The rod whined toward Kennedy's face.

He saw it coming, had anticipated it, was moving before it could land. He ducked and felt the steel tear at his hair, then had risen, his right hand gripping the slender shaft, his left reaching to trap the overseer's wrist. Unthinking reflex lifted his foot in a savage kick. The chain arrested the movement and he stumbled, falling, tearing the rod from Bauchi's hand.

He rose to see the overseer springing backward, his hand tearing at the stun-gun at his belt. A moment and the weapon would be free, its energy tearing at his nerves and rending him helpless. Kennedy lifted the rod like a spear, poised it, threw it with all the massive strength of back and shoulders. As the gun came clear, the tip of the rod smashed into the snarling mouth, breaking teeth, ripping the tongue, burying the blunt end into the spine.

Bauchi cried out, his hands lifting, keel juice and blood gushing from his mouth in streams of red and blue. He turned, took one step, then slumped lifeless to the floor.

'His gun,' snapped Kennedy. 'Quickly!'

A man threw him the weapon.

'Now the rod. Fendor!'

'I'm here.' The miner had pulled himself into the working from the tunnel. He scowled at the dead body of the guard. 'He asked for it,' he commented. 'And he deserved it. But what happens now?'

'We make our break,' snapped Kennedy. 'Strip the body and dump it into the tunnel. Then stand by and do nothing. When other guards come to see why we aren't working, show them the hole. Tell them Bauchi went through it. I'll take it from there.'

He shuffled down to the far end of the working, the stun-gun hidden beneath his shirt. He had given the rod to Fendor, who now wiped it clean and dropped it at the rim of the hole. The stage set, they could do nothing but wait.

The guards came with lifted rods, faces hard with impatient

77

anger. Three of them – ready to whip and stun and beat the slaves back to their tasks.

Their leader snapped, 'What goes on here? Get back to work at once. Back, I say, or I'll break a few bones.'

'It's Bauchi,' said Fendor quickly. 'He went through here.' He gestured toward the hole.

The guard stared at it. 'Where does it go?'

'We don't know. I was digging and the pick went right through. Bauchi came and said he'd investigate. He hasn't come back.'

One of the other guards said, 'Careful, Mocha. It could be a trap.'

He was cautious, more suspicious than the others. He stayed back, one hand on his stun-gun, his eyes searching the area. They narrowed as he saw the telltale stains.

'Mocha!' he snapped. 'Wait a minute. There's blood on the floor.'

The man whose nose Bauchi had smashed with his rod moaned and dropped his hand. His face was a mask of blood, the front of his shirt thick with crimson stains.

Mocha laughed. 'Sure there is and that's where it came from. You worry too much, Ortig.'

The guard was stubborn. 'It isn't just blood. I can smell keel juice.'

'You would.' Mocha was impatient. 'Bauchi uses it. He spits all the time. Now watch this scum while I find out what happened to him.'

He thrust his head into the opening and Kennedy saw him tense. In seconds he would see the body and give the alarm. One of the other guards had stepped deeper into the working; Ortig, the suspicious one, stayed at the end, his stun-gun halfway out of its holster.

Kennedy dropped, snatching out his own gun, firing from the floor upward so that the beam hit the man's upper torso. As Ortig fell, he rolled, firing at the second guard. He heard a yell, the whine of a rod slashing through the air, the soggy impact of its landing. Fendor, his face a mask of hatred, hit again as Mocha fell back from the opening. A third time. A fourth.

'Stop it,' snapped Kennedy. 'That's enough. He's dead. Stand by with his gun. Some of you others strip off their uniforms. Hurry!'

'What's the point of taking their clothes?' said Fendor. His face was drawn, suffused with rage. 'Let's get as many of the animals as we can before they know it.'

'We need the element of surprise,' said Kennedy impatiently. 'The uniforms will help us to get it.'

'We can't get them on with these chains.'

'We won't be wearing chains. Pass me those other two guns.'

Kennedy tore the butt plate from his own weapon. Inside rested the battery which activated the piece. He removed it, probed with his fingers, dismantling the weapon. He tore thick conducting strips from the interior and hooked them to the battery connections. Carefully he bent them and rested them against the link fastened to his left fetter. Gently he closed the strips, squinting as an arc sprang into being. Like a hot knife through butter it cut through the link. He twisted it from the staple and did the same at the other end.

He threw the crude torch to one of the men.

'Do the same for Fendor.'

He reached for another of the stun-guns and repeated the procedure. The third torch he used merely to sever the chains of the others. As the arc spluttered and died, he reached for a uniform, donned it, stood with the remaining stun-gun in his hand.

'Get dressed,' he said to the miner and two others. 'Remember that you are guards, so walk as they do. Swagger, be arrogant, use the rods if you have to.' To the others he said, 'Tie your chains together with scraps of rag. Remember to shuffle. When you have to move fast a jerk will break the bindings. But wait until I give the word.'

One said, dubiously, 'And then what? I'm willing to make a break, but how far do you think we'll get? The shift isn't over yet. They'll be suspicious the moment they see us walk out without a reason.'

'We'll have a reason,' said Kennedy. He moved toward the opening, rested his ear against the stone and listened. The grinding was very loud.

'The worm.' Fendor grinned his understanding. 'The body you left as bait. You want it to come through into the working.'

'That's right. When – ' Kennedy broke off as an angry shout came from the gallery.

'Where's the stone for processing? What's the matter up there? You having trouble?'

'No trouble,' yelled Kennedy. His voice was like Mocha's,

snarling, angry. 'These lazy scum are afraid of something. I'll teach them to be afraid. Work, you louts! Work, damn you!'

He sent the rod whining through the air. A man, quick of thought, screamed. Others followed. In seconds the air was bedlam, full of shouts, the whine of steel rods, fictitious cries of pain.

He was playing for time, but the men overdid it. Attracted by the noise, guards came running from the gallery, stun-guns in hand. Kennedy recognized the danger and ran to meet them, shouting, waving his hand down the working. Three passed him and he turned and fired, dropping them where Fendor and the others in uniform could snatch up their weapons. A fourth skidded to a halt.

'You!' he snapped. 'You're not Mocha. Where is he? What's going on?'

He stood in plain sight of a dozen others, wary, cautious, his stun-gun leveled at the tall figure standing before him.

Kennedy made a vague gesture. 'The slaves. Trouble. They've found something.' He turned, headed back toward the narrow working. 'You'd better follow me.'

'Not so fast.' The gun in the man's hand jerked a little. 'I'm not happy about this. That uniform – ' He broke off, finger tensing to fire.

Kennedy dropped him and sprang back into the working as the others opened fire. A haze of electronic energy sparkled from the stone inches before his face and he felt the numbing shock of reflected forces. For the moment he was safe; the working angled from the main gallery and before the guards could blast it they had to face the opening. But it was only a matter of time before they brought up shields and stunned everyone within.

'We're trapped,' said Fendor bitterly. 'They've got us blocked. We can't get out.' He turned as behind him a man yelled in terror. The yell died in a crashing shower of rock, rose again in naked horror. 'The worm!' Fendor whitened beneath the dust and grime on his face. 'Dear God, we're trapped between those guards and the worm!'

CHAPTER TWELVE

It came with a rush, spinning, the bands around the pointed mass tearing rock to send it in a shower of choking fragments. It reached the dead bodies of the guards, openings appearing, closing, the great mass pressing forward in a thin rain of blood and tissue. It filled the far end of the working and, before it, men ran for their lives.

'Wait!' Kennedy sprang before them, arms extended. 'Wait, you damned fools! Wait!'

The worm moved fast, but there was time. He struck out at a terrified face, the flat of his hand hard against a cheek. Another, a third. He stood a grimly determined figure, his voice rising to kill the panic which had taken hold.

'Listen to me,' he snapped. 'If you run out there, the guards will shoot you down. Is that what you want?'

'If we stay here, that thing will kill us,' yelled a man.

'If we let it, yes,' admitted Kennedy. 'But we're not going to let it. Now do as I say. Find niches and squeeze into them. Get back as far as you can. When the thing has passed, come out ready to fight for your lives.' His voice hardened into the tone of command. 'Now do it. Move, damn you! Move!'

He waited until the last moment, until all the others had found positions of safety, moving backward before the pointed head, attracting it with his scent, the promise of water and food. It had no eyes and no discernible mouth, but patches of the paler skin could be sensitive to light and the tiny openings would gulp crushed stone to feed the creature's strange metabolism. It was huge, but he had seen too many alien life-forms to be afraid. And it could be used. When the guards in the gallery saw it, they would run in screaming panic.

At the last second, he dived into an opening, forcing himself deep in the narrow crack as the creature drew level. For a moment it hesitated, the pointed snout weaving and then, attracted by what lay beyond, it forged ahead.

Kennedy saw the head pass, the spinning bands merging into

6

a rough hide like that of a giant rasp. Rock flaked from the edges of the opening, narrowing the fissure, coming closer as the worm moved onward. If the hide should touch him, it would strip the clothes from his body, the flesh from his bones, shredding him into a mass of unrecognizable tissue.

It grew dark, solid black, a darkness filled with a grinding vibration. Kennedy held his breath. If the creature should veer, if the body was larger than he had guessed, if the rock protecting him should crumble, then he would certainly die.

After what seemed to be an eternity light returned; a single radbulb had escaped being crushed, and by its light he saw the rear of the worm, the point, the bands and patches exactly the same as those in the front. Kennedy jumped from his niche. The others were waiting.

'All right,' he snapped. 'Let's go!'

Beyond the worm lay chaos. The guards had lost all discipline, running, yelling as the worm bore down the gallery. A few used their stun-guns, the weapons having no effect on the great bulk. Using it as a shield, Kennedy led his tiny force into battle.

Guards yelled, were shot down, falling stunned and helpless. Men snapped the fastenings of their chains and raced forward to pick up fallen guns, using them to stun still more guards. From an opening men came running, a familiar voice rising high.

'Cap! Over here!'

It was Arden Hensack. He held a bloodstained rod in his hand. He lashed at the head of a guard, snatched up the man's gun as he fell, and used it to down two others. Kennedy ran toward him, dodged the blast of a gun, fired back, and halted beside the other man.

'Trouble?'

'Some guards. They're trying to warn the surface.'

There were three of them, one hunched over a communicator, the others standing guard. They fired together as Kennedy ran forward. He saw the raised hands, the closing fingers, and threw himself down just in time. He triggered twice, a third time, and the gun was exhausted. With a blow of his fist he smashed the communicator from the wall.

'We've got to reach the surface,' he snapped. 'Find tools and get men to remove the chains. Organize gangs. Fendor! To me!'

The little uniformed party raced forward. Guards, utterly

82

disorganized by the worm and the sudden attack, led the way. A crowd of them thronged the elevator, too many for the doors to close.

Kennedy yelled, 'Orders from above! Form a line against the worm. Move!'

'Orders, hell!' A sweating man cursed as he tried to force his way into the elevator. 'I'm getting out of here!'

Kennedy reached forward, grabbed the man by the shoulder and sent the edge of his stiffened hand hard against the side of his neck. Throwing the unconscious man to one side, he repeated the maneuver. Fendor and the rest joined in, their guns heaping the floor with stunned men. Within minutes the area outside the elevator was covered with twitching shapes.

'We did it!' Fendor blew out his cheeks. 'By God, we did it.'

'Not yet,' snapped Kennedy. The cage was too slow, and he fumed with impatience as it moved up the shaft. A word from below, a warning that the slaves had broken free, and the upper level would be ringed with armed men.

'My gun's out,' said one of the others. 'We should have got others.'

There had been no time. Seconds counted now that they were on their way. And stun-guns would be useless against men armed with missile weapons and lasers. A bell jangled from the side of the cage.

'Trouble?' A thin voice echoed from the speaker as Kennedy pressed the button of the communicator. 'Why are you coming up?'

'No trouble,' said Kennedy quickly.

'Are you sure? There was a broken message –'

'Some rock has fallen.' Kennedy glanced up through the lattice of the roof of the cage. Another few feet and they would be at the surface. 'A few of the slaves took advantage of it and tried to make a break, but we've quietened them down. I'm coming up to make a report.'

'Then why not use –' The voice broke off as the cage came to a halt. A man sat at a desk in an open expanse surrounded with doors. He gurgled as Kennedy gripped his throat. 'What's happening? What are you doing?'

'Taking over. Where is the arsenal?'

A thin hand lifted, pointing.

'And the guards?'

'In there.' Again the man pointed.

'Who else is up here?' Kennedy's hand tightened a little. 'Quickly! I want answers and no lies.'

'Just a couple of engineers.' The man swallowed as the iron hand left his throat. 'We went into full-scale underground production. Most of the guards and supervisors are below.'

Kennedy glanced at the control panel before which the man sat. A red light winked and he thumbed a button.

'Surface?' The voice held panic. 'Send men, guns, and gas down here. All hell's broken loose. There's a thing and – ' The voice died in a scream of pain.

Other lamps shone, some stationary, others moving. The signal lights of other elevators. Kennedy operated switches and the lights shone steady as the cages came to rest. If they carried workers, they would come to no harm; if guards, they were better off trapped in the shafts.

Fendor had been busy. From the arsenal he had taken stubby machine guns, their magazines each holding a hundred explosive missiles. Grimly he nodded to the man at the door of the room which held the guards.

'Right. Open it.'

Before Kennedy could interfere, he had stepped to the open panel and blaster the interior with a rain of death. It was hard justice, savage, but well-deserved. The men inside would wield no more bone-breaking rods, gloat over no more helpless slaves.

'Get back underground,' said Kennedy as the echoes died. 'Load up with guns. If you see any guards, you know what to do.'

Fendor was grim. 'We know. And you?'

'Give me a gun. I'll stand watch up here. Find a man named Arden Hensack and send him up with a few others. They can take over. Then get the rest of the workers to the surface. You can leave the guards below.'

'For the worm,' said Fendor. 'If they dodge it, they can wait until we get them.' His voice hardened. 'Not that there will be many left.'

Kennedy moved around the area as the cage vanished down the shaft. The communications operator watched him nervously.

'Are you going to kill me?'

'Not unless I have to.' Kennedy opened the doors, checked compartments. 'Are you certain there isn't anyone else around?'

'Only the engineers and they're out on a survey. I told you, we went into full-scale production. Sina Lahari ordered it.'

That and a lot more. The guards, the rods, the slaves. Sina Lahari, thought Kennedy, would have a lot to answer for.

He jerked open a door and looked at the arid surface of the planetoid. Twenty yards ahead, rising up and back in a sweeping curve, a bubble of plastic sealed the shaft area against the void. Beyond it lay buildings, one more prominent than the rest. It stood on a low hill, the red light of the sun reflecting from broad windows. Behind it rested the slender shape of a small spaceship.

Kennedy drew in his breath.

'That building,' he snapped. 'Can it be reached by a tunnel?'

'Yes.' The man, scared, was eager to please. 'There's an underground passage leading from the engineers' quarters over there.' He gestured to where a low shed stood close to where a heap of debris glittered in the sun. 'The Baron had it dug first thing, before we raised the air-seal to cover the shaft area.'

'Good for the Baron,' said Kennedy dryly. 'I'll be paying him a visit later on.'

'Not now?'

'No. Now you just lie down on the floor, your arms extended above your head, and pretend to be dead.' Kennedy touched the thin chest with the muzzle of his machine gun. 'Try very hard. Remember – your life depends on it.'

Back at the control panel he pressed buttons, listened, heard nothing. Overriding the manual controls of the elevators, he sent the stalled cages back to the bottom. If Fendor hadn't managed to gain mastery by now, he never would.

A lamp glowed, began to rise. Kennedy hit the communicator button. 'Who are you?'

'That you, Cap?' Arden's voice echoed from the speaker. 'I'm on my way up as you ordered. I've got a dozen men with me. Can you hold on up there?'

Kennedy looked at the silent area, the lone man shivering on the floor.

'Yes,' he said. 'I can manage.'

'We've taken over down here. Fendor's got men driving the worm into a working and all the slaves are free. You did a great job, Cap! A great job!'

'It isn't finished yet,' said Kennedy.

He caught Arden by the arm as the man left the elevator cage and led him through the door into the protected area outside. Beyond the plastic film the stars shone with luminous splendor, sheets and clouds of glowing gases, spirals, shapes of occluding dust making the heavens a montage of form and pattern. Among them the ball of the dying sun looked a sullen ember.

'It's good,' said Arden, looking at the stars. 'At times, down there, I thought I'd never see a sight like this again. That I'd die down there, breathing dust, my face inches from the stone. That some sadistic swine of a guard would smash my spine for the hell of it.' His hands clenched. 'Well, we took care of them. They'll do no more slaving.'

Kennedy said nothing, letting the man enjoy his revenge.

'If it hadn't been for you, Cap, we –' Arden broke off, shaking his head. 'How do you thank a man for saving your life? For getting him out of a living hell? I said I'd heard about you. A lot of what I heard I didn't believe. I was wrong. You're as good as they say. Cap! Let me shake your hand!'

He was emotional, a fault in any agent, but he was young and suffering from reaction. Kennedy gripped the thin fingers – it was quicker than to argue.

'The job isn't over yet,' he said. 'I told you that. We've got to get to that building over there.' He pointed with the muzzle of his gun. 'There's an underground passage, so we won't be seen. But we'd better hurry.'

'The Baron,' said Arden. 'That's a man I want to meet.'

'Sina Lahari.' Kennedy led the way toward the engineers' quarters. 'Him, those behind him, that ship lying behind the building. I want them all!'

'The ship!' Arden halted, staring upward, his face strained. 'Cap! We're too late!'

CHAPTER THIRTEEN

The ship was rising. It lifted with a halo of etheric blue as the drive took hold, seeming to hang poised for a moment over the rough surface of the planetoid. And then it moved, heading up and away to where the stars shone in eye-bright splendor, to vanish in the empty dark.

'It's gone!' Arden's shoulders sagged. 'Cap! We're stranded!'

The man wasn't thinking. There would be a radio, men in the buildings, perhaps, and Kennedy had seen the bold symbol blazoned on the prow of the sleek craft.

'That was the personal ship of Elgha Zupreniz,' he snapped. 'The Lord of Sergan must have paid his world a visit. Now he's gone back home. We must hurry before those in the building get curious!'

The engineers' quarters were deserted. Kennedy looked at the compartments, the tables, charts, graphs, and plotting devices. A row of core-samples stood on a shelf. A spectroscope stood on a bench. A small grinding machine lay next to a group of acids and reagents. Beyond lay another room, smaller, the square of a trap clear in the sponge plastic of the floor. It opened to a short flight of stairs. Kennedy descended them, Arden at his heels. A rough tunnel stretched before them, the roof studded with radbulbs.

Kennedy raced down it, his eyes narrowed, searching. He caught the glint of light from metal strips to either side and halted.

'A detector,' he said, 'We'll have to leave the guns behind.'

There could be others, those designed to register the heat of their bodies, but engineers would not be carrying guns and he did not want the metal detectors to warn of their coming. Fifty feet on he saw a lens and stood before it as Arden passed. A guard could have business in the building; a slave would not. Blocking the lens was an elementary precaution.

At the end of the passage a flight of stairs led up to a trap. Kennedy reached it, thrust it open, sprang into the room above.

A door led to another room, a man who rose from behind a desk, his eyes startled.

'What –'

He fell before he could finish the question, dropping beneath the slash of Kennedy's stiffened hand. As he slumped unconscious to the floor a buzzer began to sound. A dead-hand signal activated by the guard's failure to negate the initial impulse.

Sina Lahari was a cautious man.

He stood behind his desk, very calm, one finger resting on a box before him. It was small, square, the button beneath his finger depressed to the surface.

'Be warned,' he said as Kennedy and Arden burst into the room. 'Do nothing foolish. Should pressure be removed from the button, all in the mine will die.' He gestured toward the window, the dome of airtight plastic sealing the shaft area. 'There are explosive charges set beneath the edges of the seal. I have sent the preliminary impulse. If my finger should fall from the button, or unless it is canceled, the charges will detonate.' His voice became a feral purr. 'Do I have to tell you what will happen then?'

Air, blasting from the mine, carrying with it a cloud of debris, the broken and shattered bodies of men who, if not immediately killed by the storm, would die in the airless void.

Kennedy said, tightly, 'If that happens, I will kill you.'

The Baron shrugged. 'Perhaps, if you are able, but I think it will be poor consolation. And you will not be able. That buzzer you heard is summoning men. Not those at the mine but others in this building. Already they are beyond the door.'

'I locked it,' said Arden.

'Of course, but how long will it keep them out?' Sina Lahari raised his voice a little. 'Come no closer. I warn you: the lives of all in the mine will be forfeited if you do not obey.'

It was an impasse – but one which couldn't last. Kennedy heard the pounding at the door. Soon armed men would be bursting into the office to shoot them down. Deliberately he took another step forward, counting on the Baron's greed, his reluctance to destroy the source of his wealth. And, like all cat-men, he had a healthy regard for his own skin.

'We are in an odd position,' said Kennedy. 'You can destroy the mine, but nothing can stop me killing you. And, if those guards come in here, that is exactly what I shall do.'

'The mine – '

'To hell with the mine!' Kennedy made his voice harsh, impatient. 'What are a bunch of slaves to me? Let them die and the guards with them. I'm only worried about myself.'

He took another step forward, eyes searching the box beneath Lahari's hand. To one side was another button, the canceling switch, he guessed. The Baron would never have pressed the impulse signal unless he could cancel it. If he could reach it, press it, he would have the situation under control.

He eased forward, tensing his muscles, readying them for action. The blinding speed of unthinking reflex as taught by the Clume Discipline. Against it, normal action was slow. Lahari would have to see him move, decide what to do, send a signal from his brain to the resting finger. Before it could lift, Kennedy would have pressed the canceling button – if he could get a little closer, move fast enough, act without warning.

He said, 'Let's talk about this. We've taken over the mine. Either way you lose, unless we can make a deal. You either blow it up or we destroy it. In neither case can anyone make a profit.'

'A deal?' The cat-man relaxed a little; this was language he could understand. 'What had you in mind?'

'Money. Passage to a civilized world. Your word that we won't be harmed.' Kennedy added, shrewdly, 'I could be of use to you. Chombite is valuable and I know just where to get the best price. The Regent of Lakaan, for example. He and I have done business before.'

He saw the Baron's eyes veil with thought, the agile mind behind the soft fur considering, evaluating, planning what was best to do. To agree and later to take revenge. To stall. To draw out the discussion so as to gain time for the guards to break down the door. To –

Before the decision could be made, Kennedy had acted. He moved, body thrown forward, his right hand extended toward the box. He touched the button and pressed it an instant before Lahari lifted his hand. The next second he had gripped the lithe figure, the fingers of his left hand digging at the furred throat.

'The guards,' he snapped. 'Order them to drop their arms. Now!'

Lahari choked but obeyed.

'Get their guns, Arden. Lock them in a safe place. Hurry!'

As the man did as ordered Kennedy searched the Baron. He

found a flat pistol, a thin, vicious-looking knife. Throwing the weapons to one side, he said, 'And now we'd better talk. Just where is this place?'

'You are on the world of Sergan.'

'The coordinates?'

Lahari hesitated, then gave them. It was no time to argue or to be clever. Rubbing his throat, he cursed himself for a fool. He should have left with Elgha Zupreniz, obeying the instinct which had warned him that trouble was brewing. But the temptation had been too great. Another few days, a week, a month even, and each hour would add to the heap of chombite in store. And the Lord of Sergan had been suspicious. Lahari had decided that it would be best to travel alone, to do what he had planned to do from the beginning.

But he was still alive. The big man had not killed him and the Baron had a shrewd idea that he was not exactly what he seemed.

Arden returned to the chamber. 'All safe, Cap. I've got them locked in tight. There were only three of them, four counting the one at the desk. They won't bother us.' He glanced at the Baron. 'Did you get the coordinates?'

'Yes.' Kennedy gave them. 'Is there a radio?'

'In the other room. I'd better make contact and call up some help.'

'Cap?' Lahari frowned, remembering vague rumors. 'Cap Kennedy?'

'Yes.'

'I should have guessed.' Lahari relaxed, smiling. 'You're no ordinary space-drifter. Elgha Zupreniz was right when he called you a champion. Allow me to congratulate you, my friend. Your acting was superb. For a moment there I really believed that you cared nothing for those in the mine.' He reached for a small box on the desk, removed a confection, slipped the spiced morsel into his mouth. Sucking, he added, 'So you are working for Terra. Well, well, that places an entirely different complexion on things.'

'No,' said Kennedy. 'I will kill you, if I have to.'

'Agreed, but you are not a murderer and I assure you, my friend, that I will give you no cause.' Lahari swallowed the spiced drop. 'Basically you are a law-abiding man. You strive to uphold the rules and regulations of civilization as applied to decent living. And, even if you consider things to be worse

90

than they could be, your hands are tied.' He gestured toward the window, the dome of the mine. 'What are your intentions?'

'To put an end to this vileness. To free the workers. To make you pay.'

'With my life?' Lahari shrugged. 'I think not.'

'You will pay,' said Kennedy harshly. 'Those workers will get compensation. More will be paid to the installations ruined by your order. You'll pay, Baron, to the last scrap of your wealth.'

'I have no wealth.' Lahari sat down, relaxed, smiling, a little amused. 'You are forgetting something. I am merely a servant of the Lord of Sergan. He rules this world and he has absolute power. Sergan is an autonomous state. No matter what has been done and no matter how you might decry it, there is nothing you can do. In fact, at this very moment, you are guilty of rebellion against a recognized government. Should you escape, Elgha Zupreniz has the right to ask the aid of every friendly power to apprehend you and return you to his jurisdiction.' His voice softened a little, purring. 'And, my friend, a man who possess a source of chombite has many, many friends.'

Kennedy drew in his breath. 'The slaves?'

'Were purchased from various traders. How they obtained them is no concern of ours. On Sergan it is not a crime to purchase slaves or anything else which might be offered for sale. Of course, some governments could ask for compensation and, if their case is just, we might even pay it. But we cannot be held responsible for the actions of despicable pirates and greedy men who operated on their own behalf. They are the concern of the worlds to which they belong. It is no part of the policy of Sergan to police this sector of space.'

Sina Lahari leaned back in his chair, one hand reaching for the box of confections. 'You would care to join me? No? As you wish. I find a small pleasure in the tang of spice, but others may have other tastes. However, there is one taste which all find objectionable. The taste of defeat. You see, my friend, you cannot win. And, in case you are wondering. I am an attested noble of the court of Sergan. All I have done was beneath the direction of Elgha Zupreniz. If there is blame, it is his. If there are matters to be answered to, then he must answer them. No government in the galaxy would blame a loyal and dedicated servant for obeying the commands of his ruler. To do so would be to invite anarchy.'

He savored the spice drop, enjoying the moment. From the beginning he had anticipated such an eventuality, remote though it had seemed. And now his foresight was bringing its reward. The cases of gems he had sent to Obrac, the rich fruits of the mine carefully hidden, would be there for later collection. The few he had given Elgha Zupreniz for show, to provide ready cash and to keep the fool quiet, were but a fraction of those torn from the planetoid. Wealth undreamed of, waiting his pleasure.

Added insurance in case of need.

Arden came into the room. He was strained, anxious.

'Cap! I think you'd better get on the radio.'

'Can't you make contact?'

'Yes, but – ' Arden broke off, making a helpless gesture. 'I've heard it, but I don't believe it. Maybe you can talk sense into the fool. I can't.'

'May I accompany you?' Lahari rose. 'This should be most interesting.'

The screen was alive with color. The face of Commander Sukarno strained with tearing frustration. He held the power, to destroy a world, ships and men enough to wage a planetary war, but he was helpless.

'It's diplomacy, Cap. You're operating in an area so sensitive that one wrong move could start a debacle. I checked with Terra and they're worried sick. The rumor is out that a new source of chombite has been found. Every petty ruler wants to get in on the game and every damn one of them is rattling a saber.'

'Let them.' Kennedy was curt. 'You've forces enough to take over. Send in ships and men and do it. Call it a rescue operation if you have to, but get here fast!'

Sukarno drew in his breath. 'Don't tempt me, Cap,' he pleaded. 'I want to do just that, but I daren't. Too many eyes are watching. If we move in, it will be construed as an invasion. An act of war against an autonomous planet. Ships are sniffing around like dogs circling a bone. If we move in, they will follow us. If we take over, they will form a combine to protect the official ruler of Sergan. They don't give a damn about him, of course, but the excuse will be good enough. By the time the fuss

92

has died, we'll have a full-scale space war on our hands. From then on it's anyone's guess as to how things will turn out.' He paused, then added, 'It's a hell of a situation, Cap. I can't see any way out of it. Can you?'

From where he stood at the edge of the screen Lahari said, softly, 'There is no way out, my friend. But we can compromise. A while ago you asked for money, passage to a civilized world, and my word that you would not be harmed. You may have what you asked for. Wealth enough to make you rich. And, if you want even more, the Lord of Sergan will make you a noble.'

He held, he thought, all the cards. No power wanted a rival to gain the source of chombite, and each would fight to gain a place as the protector of the tiny world. To play both ends against the middle, to set one against the other was, he knew, the path to quick riches, the maintenance of power and position. While the dogs snarled, the bone was safe.

Kennedy said, with quick decision, 'Send me a ship. A small one, harmless, with some men to back me up. Can you do that?'

'A small ship, yes.'

'Then move the rest of your forces as close as you dare. Have them ready and standing by.'

'I can't come in, Cap,' insisted Sukarno. 'I can't even set down a rescue party without the permission of the accepted ruler of Sergan.'

'Just send the small ship.' Kennedy glanced at the Baron. He wase smiling, gloating over the impasse. 'No, wait. I've a better idea. Forget the ship.'

'Good,' Sukarno grunted his relief. 'I'll send it if you want it, Cap, but it's taking a chance. Can you manage without?'

'Yes. Stand by until you hear from me.'

'A man of wisdom,' commented Lahari as the screen died. 'It is better not to let others know what you intend. You will accept my offer?'

'Perhaps.' Good advice should be taken. Kennedy turned to Arden. 'Take over here. Get the men out of the mine and clean up the mess. Keep them working if you can. Tell them they're on high pay with a bonus due for past tribulation. Get Fendor to help you; he'll know what to do.'

'And you, Cap?'

Kennedy smiled. 'I'm taking a little trip. The Baron is going to summon a ship from Obrac and we are going to see the Lord

93

of Sergan.' His smile grew wider, but his eyes remained hard, cold, and utterly ruthless. 'There is something I have to say to him.'

CHAPTER FOURTEEN

The Lord of Sergan was enjoying himself. He sat on a low dais, glittering in his gilded mail, his crest, a vivid blue. One clawed hand gripped a goblet of wine, the other a joint of meat. Between drinking and eating he stared at the arena below.

The croat was in trouble. The thing backed, claws lifted, ichor oozing from a dozen wounds. Two legs had been torn from the armored body and the thorax was cracked. Another attack, he thought, two at the most, and the bout would be over. The Fenedish clan humbled. The tharg he had managed to buy from Dulen Yanchiga the undisputed victor.

A servant refilled his goblet. 'A masterly show, my lord,' he whispered. 'Never have I seen the like. Your name will be praised both in the palace and in the city.'

Negligently Elgha Zupreniz waved the joint of meat.

'A small thing,' he said. 'But not without interest. It pleases me to entertain my friends.'

'Your friends and humble followers, my lord.' The servant bowed. 'If I might be so bold as to request a place in your retinue?'

'I'll think about it.'

'I would be honored, sire.'

Elgha Zupreniz swelled at the use of the title. More and more men were flattering his vanity, giving him the deference which was long overdue. From a servant it was nothing, a man seeking a better position, but it showed the way the wind was blowing. And trust those who lurked in the shadows to know where true power lay. Now his brothers ruled Obrac, an uneasy alliance held only by mutual interest. They had little wealth and what they had they saved for useless purposes. New roads, more

94

jungle cleared, fields prepared for crops. A river had been dammed and a mine started. There was talk of inviting manufacturers to Obrac to open new fields of industry.

Weakness which held the seeds of destruction. The Ghazen were a warrior race and needed little but food, wine, and the thrill of combat. Money could provide them all and he had money and to spare. There was no need of off-worlders to build their factories. No need of new fields and roads. The people wanted the arena and the sport it could provide and, with the wealth of chombite, he could give them that and more.

And then, when his popularity was high enough, when more than servants gave him the title reserved only for the rulers of Obrac, then would come his hour.

He threw aside the meat, rising as the crowd roared. The tharg, trailing a broken limb, its hide gaping in a score of places, lunged to the attack. Great jaws opened, closed, the coat twisting, clashing its claws as teeth tore at the junction of thorax and abdomen. Ichor spilled to the sand, the grains pluming beneath the gust of air from the ventricles.

Hysterically a man screamed, 'A thousand to one on the tharg!'

He was ignored as everything was ignored save the drama in the arena. The tharg moved in for the kill. Fangs gleamed, vanished in gushes of ichor, ripped at yielding chiton. The croat threshed, twisted, and fell into two parts. Incredibly the claws continued to snap.

A yell announced the victory. Beaming, Elgha Zupreniz rose, arms lifted, his bull-roar rising above the shouts.

'There will be wine,' he boomed. 'And food. Eat, drink and be merry. Thus it was in the old days. So it will be again.'

A man called, 'When you rule Obrac, my lord?'

'The Lord of Sergan, King of Obrac!' yelled another. 'Long life to Elgha Zupreniz!'

Others caught up the cry, repeated it, their voices like drums as they echoed from the ringed enclosure. It was heady stuff, stronger than wine, the primitive beat of warriors calling to their chief. Almost Elgha Zupreniz was tempted to bring it to a head, to put his future to the test and lead a march on the Palace. Saner considerations prevailed, the lessons hard-learned from Baron Sina Lahari. To be cautious, to wait, to hit only when there was no chance of failure.

And yet it was hard to resist.

Back home, he bathed and had sweet oils rubbed into his scales. Dressed in a flowing robe of crimson, his crest a soft, satisfied azure, he summoned a servant.

'What reports from Sergan?'

'The usual, my lord. Production high, the slaves under control, everything as it should be.'

The servant was casual. He had not recognized Arden on the screen; to him almost all humans looked alike.

'Reestablish contact. I want to talk to the Baron.'

He sat brooding as the servant obeyed. It was time to prepare and, to do it, he needed all the gems he could get. Production had been disappointing, the first satisfaction replaced by a mounting impatience. To bribe the people, to win the guards to his side, to make sure that when he ousted his brothers he would remain firmly in control, would require much wealth. Perhaps he should take a more personal interest in the mine. Lahari was good but, after all, he was only a trader. There could be others, men with more push and drive who would double the output from the slaves. Perhaps he should open a second shaft, double the number of workers? Macau Grimbach would have no trouble in filling his needs.

And he should make alliances. Without ships or heavy armament Sergan was vulnerable to raiders. The Tyrant of Telgash, perhaps? The twin rulers of Kobold? Certainly the Despot of the Dieemar Region. Gems would buy their support.

He stretched and, as the servant returned, snapped, 'I do not like to be kept waiting. Is the Baron on the screen?'

'No, my lord. He is not on Sergan.'

'What?'

'He summoned a vessel, my lord. It landed while you were at the arena and the Baron is now on Obrac.'

'Then where is he?'

'I do not know, my lord.' The servant added, 'There was also a message from the Palace. Your presence is requested at a banquet.'

'At what time?'

'Midnight, my lord. Your brothers apologize for the short notice, but stress the urgency of the matter. They wish to know if you will attend.'

The man was a fool. The seat of power lay at the Palace and that was where he should be. Elgha Zupreniz roared for servants to attend him, then barked his answer.

'Of course I will attend! Have my litter ready, ten guards, armed and in their finest livery. No, wait! Make it twenty. We have to remember our station.'

On the way he brooded behind the drawn curtains, wondering why he should have been summoned. The shouting in the arena would have carried far beyond the confines of the enclosure. Spies would have told of his popularity. His brothers could be getting worried, eager to placate, a person they had once despised. Well, he would show them. He would listen to what they had to say, weigh it, take time over his decision. They most likely needed his wealth for their stupid schemes. He might even give it – at a price.

Elgha Zupreniz, he thought happily. Lord of Sergan, King of Obrac – and who could tell where it might end?

The litter halted at the steps of the palace as he descended, a resplendent figure in golden, ceremonial mail, the harness studded with gems, the hilts of swords and dagger winking flashing radiance, the butt of the gun engraved and sparkling with precious stones. Attended by his escort, he strode up the stairs toward the great portals, shoulders back, crest high and tinged with blue, a magnificently barbaric creature eager to taste the sweet fruits of success.

To Kennedy he was nothing but a beast.

The mail meant nothing, the gems, the glowing fabrics, the gilded claws and fangs. Beneath it all lay a violent savage without thought or consideration for anything but his own desires. The blood of men had paid for the gems on hands and harness, their sweat and pain and despair the gold of the mail, the other outward signs of wealth. For a moment, looking at the strutting figure, Kennedy felt a wash of anger, a mounting fury which caused his hands to clench, the heart to pound within his chest.

'Look at it!' Fendor's voice was a snarl. 'An animal dressed as a man.' His hand dropped to his belt. 'I'd like to spill his guts.'

'No!' Kennedy's voice was low, harsh. 'Try it and I'll break your neck. This has to be played my way.'

He looked around. Fendor had refused to be left behind and had insisted on accompanying Kennedy with a half-dozen others as escort. To save argument Kennedy had agreed, and it had been a wise decision. The culture of Obrac was run on tradition, and a man of importance was never unattended, so the four men he had retained, though a small group, had made an impression. The others were with the Baron, guarding him close.

Fendor whispered, 'I've never seen anything like this before, Cap. I'm glad we're armed.'

Weapons were essential to a warrior culture; without them no man could have his pride. As they passed into the banquet hall, they were surrounded by Ghazenians in traditional harness, tall Acheons with feathered headdresses armed with long pikes, squat Chanchi with spiked clubs. Guests invited by the ruling brothers, a little uneasy at carrying unfamiliar weapons but all adding to the brightness and variety of the gathering.

Ushers guided them to a lower table, out of sight of the upper board. A gong roared its brazen note and the banquet commenced.

There were eight kinds of meat, seven of fowl, a dozen of vegetable and a score of different wines. Great platters heaped with fruit stood next to sweet confections, pastries shaped in the forms of castles, ships of space, monstrous beasts. Pipes, drums, and flutes provided wailing music, and a troupe of Boddari dancers undulated in suggestive abandon.

'This is good, Cap.' Fendor burped over his plate. 'I'd forgotten what decent food tastes like.'

'Don't eat too much of it.' Kennedy glanced at the others. 'That goes for you too. We've all starved for too long. Guzzle now and you'll get cramps. And stay off the wine.'

He toyed with a goblet of water, the leg of a fowl, eating slowly, watching, waiting as the noise increased. The dancers left to be replaced by a trio of jugglers. An eel-like thing sang a plaintive air. A feathered creature cavorted in a circle of fire. Two Ghazenians started to quarrel and were parted by armored guards.

It was time.

Kennedy rose, jerking his head at the others. In a compact group they marched toward the upper table, Kennedy in the lead, the others two by two beside and a little behind. Ahead he could see the six brothers who ruled, the crest-crowns of Obrac reflecting the light. Beside them sat Elgha Zupreniz.

Kennedy halted before him. A brimming goblet of wine stood on the board. He picked it up and with a quick movement dashed the contents into the scaled features.

'You – ' The Lord of Sergan rose, hand clawing at his harness. 'You dare – '

98

'Hold!' The whip-crack of Kennedy's voice stilled the dancers, the pipes and flutes and drums. In the silence he said, 'I challenge you. Scum of a degraded world, I challenge your right to rule!'

Elgha Zupreniz dashed wine from his slotted eyes.

'I recognize you. How dare you challenge me? You, a slave.'

'No slave,' said Kennedy sharply. 'You claimed me as your champion, remember? I have received injustice at your hands and, by the traditions of this world, I claim my right. Fight or be known for the coward you are. Your crest removed, your claws, your talons. Go branded as a thing of shame. By the laws and traditions of your race I demand satisfaction.'

'You? Demand satisfaction from me? The Lord of Sergan!'

One of the six kings moved, his claws making small sounds on the table.

'Of course, Elgha, you don't have to fight. As the ruler of your own world you can refuse. In that case, however – ' He shrugged, leaving the rest unsaid.

Another added, 'It would seem that the claimant has some genuine cause to challenge. To be taken and forced to work in a mine against his will would offend any civilized being. Still, it is up to you.'

A third said, 'In all such combats to the death the contestants enter the arena without weapons. It hardly seems fair in this case as the creature has no scales, no talons, and hardly any fangs to speak of. Yet, it is his right to commit suicide if he so wishes. That is if you agree to meet him, of course.'

Elgha Zupreniz snarled his anger. They were all against him. In fact, they had probably invited him to the banquet so that this soft creature could issue his stupid challenge. He could refuse, but if he did his popularity would be gone. He, a Ghazen, to run from a personal challenge! He would be ostracized, jeered at, and even if the full penalties were not enforced he would never be welcome on Obrac again.

He would be forced to wander among strong strange worlds, alone, despised. No female would mate with him. He would sire no line.

He had no choice but to fight. Even so an element of caution remained.

'You are brave,' he said to Kennedy. 'Foolishly so. You cannot hope to win. Yet I will be merciful. At the sight of first blood the combat will be over.'

Fendor whispered, 'Cap! Don't be crazy! Take the chance while you've got it!'

Kennedy ignored him. He said, loudly, 'I am not a coward. I ask no mercy and I shall give none. We fight to the death under the traditions of this world. Winner take all. Your life, your goods, your position against mine. If you are afraid, say so now so that all may know just what you are!'

Elgha slammed his hand on the table. Goblets jumped, spilling wine.

He roared. 'No creature calls me a coward! By the egg of my ancestors I shall rip you apart. We fight at dawn!'

'No,' said Kennedy. 'At noon!'

CHAPTER FIFTEEN

The arena was like an oven, the sun burning down from overhead, the sand hot beneath his naked feet, the very air seeming to be the breath of a furnace. Naked aside from shorts, Kennedy squinted against the glare as Fendor rubbed oil into his skin.

'You're crazy,' he muttered. 'You should have fought at dawn. It would have been cooler then. You wouldn't be roasting in this damned heat.'

Kennedy glanced around. Under the awnings the crowd waited, watchful, tense with expectation. At the far end of the arena Elgha Zupreniz suffered the ministrations of his old pit-master. Like Kennedy, he was naked aside from vivid crimson shorts. His scaled body caught the light, the oil reflecting the glare in rainbow shimmers. His crest glowed blue as he flexed his muscles. The doubts of the previous night had gone; now he was confident of a quick, easy victory.

'I shall rake at his eyes,' he said. 'When he flinches, I'll rip out his guts with a foot. The fool doesn't stand a chance.'

Th pit-master grunted. 'I've seen him in action, master; you haven't. He's quick and strong.'

100

'True.' The Lord of Sergan remembered how Kennedy had bested the alien creature aboard the *Quell*. 'But he is soft. That flesh will rip at a touch.' He lifted his hands. The talons had been filed to needle points. He flexed them, jaws wide in a savage grin. 'I'll kill him and throw his entrails to my brothers. Then let us see how much longer they will rule Obrac.'

A gong clashed, the throbbing note rising in fading echoes. Fendor slapped his hand on the naked shoulder.

'Good luck, Cap. If – '

'You know what to do.'

'Sure, but – ' Fendor broke off. 'Hell, it isn't going to happen. Get in there and give him hell!'

The gong throbbed again and a guard gestured for the miner to leave. A third time and Kennedy was alone.

He moved slowly, taking his time, the sand hot beneath his feet, the sun on his body. It was no whim that he had chosen noon as the time of combat. Beneath their awnings the crowd had protection against the blazing sun, but Elgha Zupreniz had no such shelter. He was descended from lizard stock and Kennedy knew he could not sweat like a man. High temperatures would make him sluggish, would kill if continued. All his other combats had been set at the cool of dawn; only beasts fought during the day.

'Are you afraid, little man? Having second thoughts? Don't worry; you will not linger. Death will come quickly – that I promise.'

He strutted, playing to the crowd, wasting energy. Kennedy let him do it. He was fighting for survival, not to create a spectacle. His survival and the solution of a problem which threatened galactic peace. The only answer to the impasse.

He tripped and fell, apparently by accident, but when he rose he had sand clutched in both hands. He moved again, slowly, slowly, adding to the other's impatience to be done. The longer he could stay in the heat, the better would be his chances. Beneath the oil he felt sweat dew his body. Drops stung his eyes. He shook his head, felt the vibration of pounding feet, and darted aside as Elgha Zupreniz rushed toward him.

The Ghazenian turned, snarling, talons lifted high. Again he charged and again Kennedy dodged. A third time, a fourth. From the crowd came a mutter, the ugly sound of jeers.

'For you, my friend,' panted the Lord of Sergan. 'They have come to see blood, not the agility of a dancer. You must – '

He charged without warning, splayed feet kicking at the dust, hands and claws extended. Kennedy threw the sand, dropped, felt the wind as the hands slammed together just above his head. Rolling, he kicked, the sole of his bare foot aimed at a knee. It was like kicking at the bole of a tree. He rolled again, quickly as a foot lifted to rip at his side. He felt the touch of claws and, when he rose, blood streamed from a lacerated thigh.

'Clever,' snarled Elgha Zupreniz. Inner membranes had cleared his eyes of the stinging grit. 'But an old trick and not unanticipated. If you hope to live, you must do better than that.'

Kennedy backed, watchful. His opponent was agile and used to combat. The thick hide would protect vital nerve centers and his natural weaponry gave him a tremendous advantage. Against him, Kennedy had only his muscles, his hands, his quick-thinking brain. That and the training it had taken years to master.

He waited, poised on the balls of his feet, waiting for the other to attack. Always the defender had an advantage, assuming that he was not taken unawares. As the Ghazenian reached toward him, he stepped forward, gripped the scaled wrist, turned and heaved the massive weight over his shoulder.

The crowd roared.

They yelled as Elgha Zupreniz climbed to his feet, weaving a little, shaking his head. The heat was beginning to take effect. He was slower than he had been, his eyes a little vague, but Kennedy had not escaped unharmed. The free hand had ripped at his shoulder and blood ran from thin gashes down his arm and side.

Quickly he ran in, chopped down with the stiffened edge of his hand, a blow which would shatter bricks. He felt the impact, turned as an arm lifted, grabbed wrist and bicep and heaved. A foot lifted, kicking backward before he could break the arm. Releasing the bicep, he smashed his fist at the slavering jaw, breaking a fang and almost breaking a knuckle. Again he dodged a kick, saw the free hand sweep toward him, and sprang back as needle points raked his chest.

As they passed, he returned to the attack. Jumping high so as to avoid the kicking feet, trapping the arm between his chest and the scaled torso, holding himself by the left arm which he had wrapped around the blocky neck. He hit twice, felt the free hand rise to tear the flesh from his spine and jerked backward, landing on his back, continuing the movement in a complete somersault to rise and dodge away.

At the far end of the arena he paused, chest heaving, feeling the sting of multiple wounds. Blood ran from shoulder, thigh and torso, dappling his body and staining the sand. The heat fogged his eyes and Kennedy knew that he had to end the contest and soon.

Carefully he edged forward, eyes on the Lord of Sergan. The huge figure was staggering, the shoulders straightening with a visible effort, the slotted eyes dull in the scaled face. Saliva dripped from the gaping jaws. He lifted both hands as Kennedy approached.

'Now!' he boomed. 'Let us make an end!' His laughter held a sneer. 'Does the prospect of death scare you so much? Even now I will be merciful. Yield and I will spare your life.'

A trick, and Kennedy knew it. Bait dangled to make him careless, to bring him within reach of the extended talons. But two could play at psychological warfare.

He said, 'Do you mean that, my lord?'

'I do.' Elgha Zupreniz lowered his hands. Let the soft thing approach and he would rip out the guts. A quick kill and then the blessed shade, cooling sprays, surcease from the murderous heat. He felt a grim satisfaction as Kennedy came closer. Another three yards, two even, and he would attack.

Kennedy beat him to it. He raced forward with an explosion of energy, feet lifting, legs straightening, his entire body like a thrown spear. His heels slammed against the scaled torso, throwing Elgha Zupreniz back to crash supine on the sand. Before he could recover, Kennedy was on him.

Each hand gripped a wrist, holding the savage talons well away from his body. His soles jammed against the clawed feet as the top of his head slammed under the gaping jaw. Beneath his mouth he could see the softer skin of the throat, the pulsing artery beneath the tough hide. His teeth closed above it.

Under him, the scaled body surged in frantic desperation, muscles bunching, sinews like strands of steel. Grimly Kennedy held on, arms and legs like bars of iron. If he should lose his grip, allow the creature to use an arm or foot, he would be dead. Muscles knotted in his jaws as he tore at the scaled hide, using the only weapon left to him. He tasted blood, bit deeper, felt sinew against his teeth and bit again. Blood spurted against his face, filling his eyes, his nose. He turned his head, fighting for breath, feeling the warmth and splash of the pulsing fountain.

And then there was nothing he could do but wait.

Wait and summon every last scrap of his energy to hold onto the threshing shape. To resist the jerk and surge of writhing muscle. Wait until the struggles had died, until the blood ceased, until the huge shape had bled to death on the sand.

Dimly he heard the roar of the crowd, the frantic shouting, the yells of approbation. He rose, trembling, overstrained muscles jerking beneath his skin. Objects fell around him, rings, purses, ornamented daggers. The tribute of those beneath the awnings. Attendants came running to collect them in baskets. With them was Fendor and one of the kings of Obrac.

'You did it! Cap, you did it!' Fendor sucked in his breath. 'I didn't think – none of us thought – hell, Cap! Listen to the crowd!'

The roar held satiated blood-lust, the satisfaction of seeing the impossible achieved. Alive Elgha Zupreniz had won a growing popularity, dead his victor gained more. The harsh reality of a warrior-world.

Denec Zupreniz hid his satisfaction. It was not the time or place to gloat, but things had worked out very well. The troublesome younger brother was dead and no blame could be laid on the present rulers. There would be no cabal, no rebellion, no shifting of power. But tradition demanded certain formalities.

He lifted a hand and, as the roar died, said, 'I announce the victor. Elgha Zupreniz is dead, slain by the man before you. To him go the fruits of victory. The goods, the possessions, the position. All hail to the new Lord of Sergan!'

CHAPTER SIXTEEN

Commander Sukarno frowned and said, 'Well, now, Cap. I don't know.'

'You do know. You've been told. You've had the kings of Obrac tell you. They recognize me as the new Lord of Sergan. Get the lead out and get moving!'

Still the commander hesitated. 'I'd like to. There's nothing I'd like more. But Terra – '

'To hell with Terra!' Kennedy had bathed, soothing unguents easing his wounds, but they still burned and did nothing to give him patience. 'Listen,' he snapped. 'I am the recognized Lord of Sergan. The planetoid is my property and I have complete autonomy. Are you arguing about that?'

'Well, no, but – '

'As the sovereign power I am making an official request for your forces to protect my domain.'

'Take over, you mean?'

'No.' Kennedy was firm. 'I'm not giving you a free gift. All I want is for you to move in and keep others out. There is trouble at the mine,' he added. 'We are in distress. I am asking you to mount a rescue operation. I am also asking for your protection in case of invasion or attack. Damn it,' he snapped. 'How many more reasons do you want?'

Sukarno grinned. 'None. All right, Cap. I'll do it. Terra can argue about it later. All I know is that an official request has been made by the recognized authority of Sergan to give aid and protection.' He paused, then added, wonderingly, 'But, Cap, how the hell did you manage it?'

'I won a fight.'

Kennedy broke the connection and turned from the transmitter. He felt jumpy, ill at ease. His mouth held the taste of hide, blood, and gristle and he was uncomfortably aware of how slender had been the margin of victory. If a hand or foot had slipped, if he hadn't weakened his opponent by keeping him exposed to the hot sun, if Elgha Zupreniz had taken a little longer to die –

Kennedy shook his head, irritated at himself for brooding on the past. The battle was over, the thing was done, he had broken the impasse in the only way possible. But there were still matters to be taken care of.

To Fendor he said, 'Where's the Baron?'

'I don't know.' The miner frowned. 'I sent Pell to get him. They should be here by now. I'd better go after them.'

'We'll both go,' said Kennedy. He was in no mood to sit and wait. There were things he wanted to say to Sina Lahari.

He had been held under guard in a small house close to the field, apparently calm and resigned to the inevitable. He had asked for comfits, wine, and a dish of meat. And he had commented on the dilapidation of the house. But it was snug, with barred windows and a heavy door which could be barred. The safest prison Kennedy could find at short notice.

But now the door was open, a dead man lying within.

'Pell!' Fendor stooped, examining the body. The tufted feathers of a dart blotched the roundness of a cheek. 'Murdered! Shot with a dart gun!'

'Inside!' Kennedy sprang through the open door, eyes narrowed as he searched interior. A flight of steps led to an upper room where Sina Lahari had been held. At their feet lay another dead man. The door above was ajar.

It slammed back beneath Kennedy's weight. Inside was a shambles. The bottle was broken, the jagged ends smeared with blood. The dish of meat lay scattered between and beneath two other figures. One was dead, the other dying.

'He tricked us.' The voice was raw, sharp with pain as the dying man stared up at Kennedy. 'The Baron tricked us. He pretended that he was ill. When we came in he attacked us with the bottle. He smashed Elmay's skull and then – ' He coughed, blood oozing from his mouth, his slashed throat.

'There were three of you,' snapped Kennedy. 'What happened to the other man?'

'There was someone at the door. He went to see what it was. That was just as the Baron called for help. I don't know just – ' The eyes veiled, brightened a little. 'I heard something. A man. He called out and the Baron answered. And there was a name. Si – Sin – '

'Sincet?'

'It could have been that. They talked of a ship. Said something about escape. I couldn't – ' The voice died, the head falling back, sightless eyes staring at the warped panels of the ceiling.

'He's dead.' Fendor sucked in his breath. 'Four good men all dead. Pell must have bumped into them as they were on their way out. Sincet must have shot him down.'

'Yes,' said Kennedy.

'Four good men,' said Fendor again. He looked at his clenched hands. 'When I get my hands on the Baron they'll have company.'

'First we have to find him.' Kennedy led the way to the door. 'Come on; let's get to the field.'

It was a broad space at the edge of the town, ringed with a

106

perimeter fence and flanked by a tower, the humped bulk of warehouses, sheds, and repair shops. Hangars for small aircraft lay next to a row of suppliers. Space traffic was light on Obrac and the field served a double purpose.

Three ships lay on the impacted dirt: the vessel in which they had arrived on the planet, a clumsy freighter, and a sleek craft, the sides swollen with the bulk of missile launchers. A rover, a fast, vicious ship which could probe into unknown regions.

The hatch was open, rounded-headed Liganians standing guard, others busy loading a heap of supplies. Among them stood a slight figure, with peaked ears, fur soft on face and head.

'That isn't the Baron.' Fendor halted, breath rasping in his throat. They had run all the way from the house. 'It must be the other one, Sincet.'

'They'll be together,' said Kennedy. 'Sina Lahari is probably within the ship.'

'If he is, how do we get him out?' Fendor's voice sharpened. 'Cap! Look out!'

The cat-man had seen them. He turned, lifting one arm, and from his hand shot a thread of fire. It hit a yard from where they stood, exploding in a gush of flame.

He fired again as they dived for cover, a stream of missiles tearing the dirt as they crouched behind a pile of boxes.

'He's got us cornered.' Fendor peered around the edge of a box, his own pistol in his hand. Bitterly he swore. 'I can't see him from here. The angle's wrong. Maybe if I move forward a little?'

Fire burst inches above his head. Fendor cried out and clapped a hand to his face. Blood oozed around a thick splinter imbedded in his cheek. Kennedy pulled him back, dragged it out with a jerk, cautiously lifted his head.

The supplies had been abandoned, the Liganians nowhere to be seen. As he watched, the hatch began to rise. With a lithe movement Sincet jumped within the closing port.

Mockingly he called, 'Good-bye, my Lord of Sergan. Within seconds we leave, never, I hope, to meet again.'

Kennedy sprang upright. To one side rested a small aircraft, the engine humming, a little group of Ghazenians standing, numbed by the firing, the naked show of violence which they had not expected and could not understand.

They scattered as Kennedy lunged through them. He reached the door of the control cabin, grabbed the pilot by the arm, and hauled him from his seat. As the man hit the dirt, Kennedy sprang into the cabin, slammed the door, and rested his hands on the controls. They were simple, a wheel which could be turned mounted on a pillar which could be moved forward, back, and to either side. A throttle to govern power, a lever to adjust the lift of the gravity-nullifying conductors.

He threw it back to gain maximum lift, matching it with the throttle to gain maximum power, then drew back the wheel and hurtled into the sky.

Through the transparent canopy he looked at the sleek spaceship. It seemed to quiver, the halo of its drive dimmed by the sun, the etheric field softening the outlines so that the vessel seemed to be under a few inches of water. It was about to rise, to lift its pointed nose toward the void which was its natural element.

When it did, Kennedy had to be ready.

He lightly touched the controls, sending his light craft up and around in a tight circle. He would have only seconds to act, only one chance to succeed. And, even if he did not fail, there was no assurance that he would not forfeit his life.

Eyes narrowed, he concentrated on the ship below. The mass rose a trifle, lifted higher, the nose rising as it left the ground. Higher, higher still, the nose aiming toward the zenith. A normal, textbook takeoff using plenty of power and optimum angle of climb.

Kennedy hit the null-grav lever and threw it to neutral. Both hands of the wheel he pressed forward, sending the craft into a steep dive, using momentum to add to the normal weight. Before him he saw the nose of the spaceship. It was moving fast, the great engines hurling the mass of the vessel toward the sky. Around him the air screamed past the cabin. Metal tore and a wind blasted about him. Tight-lipped, he made the final adjustment.

Like a stone, the flimsy craft smashed against the nose of the rising spaceship.

The impact was relatively minor, the plating unharmed, the paint barely scratched. But a rising spaceship is in delicate balance. The impact disturbed it. The nose swung down, aiming, not at the sky, but at the ground.

The engines did the rest.

In the air Kennedy was fighting for his life. The aircraft, smashed, broken, fell like a crippled bird. He threw the null-grav to maximum lift, managed to gain a measure of control, and hit with a grinding rip of metal.

'Cap!' Fendor's face looked anxiously through the shattered canopy.

'I'm all right.' Painfully Kennedy eased himself from the wreckage. His legs hurt, his shoulder, and there was a grating pain in his chest. Broken ribs, he guessed, but at least they hadn't pierced the lung. He could walk and would be healed and soon would be fit again.

But the spaceship was finished.

'Hell,' said Fendor. 'What a mess.'

The hull was split, the control room opened out like a burst paper bag. Inside was blood and death, the Liganians, the pilot still strapped in his chair, Sincet, the Baron. The ship had been small, little more than an armed yacht, and the planet had been unyielding.

Kennedy looked at the slumped figure, the matted fur on face and head. The eyes were open; Sina Lahari had known to the last what was to come.

'He asked for it,' said Fendor. 'And you gave it to him. Cap, I never thought it could be done. I figured he was safe and snug and on his way.' He dabbed at the wound on his cheek. 'He did too, I guess.'

Safe and with an immense fortune to enjoy, Kennedy looked at the boxes which had spilled from the hold. Tough containers strapped with bands of steel. One had split and he saw the rainbow splendor of gems. Chombite from the mine, saved, hoarded, and stored until the time was right and it could be safely removed.

The gems which had rightfully belonged to Elgha Zupreniz. And which now belonged to him, the new Lord of Sergan.

He would sell them to Terra and the forces of Earth would protect his tiny world. Fendor would run it and perhaps others who had been taken there as slaves. They would receive high pay for their work and compensation for past injuries. And other debts would be paid. Macau Grimbach, for one. Kennedy knew they would meet again.

Fendor drew in his breath as he saw the precious stones.

'Look at that, Cap! And they're all yours. The mine too.' Then he added, thoughtfully, 'I guess that makes you one of the richest men in the galaxy.'

'Yes,' said Kennedy. 'I suppose it does.'

Another title in the MEWS series

F.A.T.E. 1:
Galaxy of the Lost

by Gregory Kern

Captain Kennedy, Earth's trouble shooter, carries the Banner of Terran against the unknown sciences and alien psychologies of a thousand worlds.

The crack in the cosmos that has to be sealed!

F.A.T.E. is the space hero series that has become a must wherever Science Fiction is read. A solid space adventure more exciting than 'Startrek' and far more real than 'Perry Rhodan'.

On sale at newsagents and booksellers everywhere.

MEWS BESTSELLERS

R 9   **JOHN EAGLE 1: NEEDLES OF DEATH** *Paul Edwards* 40p

R 17   **SATAN SLEUTH 1: FALLEN ANGEL** *Michael Avallone* 40p

R 25   **SPIDER 1: DEATH REIGN OF THE VAMPIRE KING**
                                                      Grant Stockbridge 40p

R 92   **SPIDER 2: HORDES OF THE RED BUTCHER**
                                                      Grant Stockbridge 40p

R 33   **FATE 1: GALAXY OF THE LOST** *Gregory Kern* 40p

R106   **FATE 2: SLAVESHIP FROM SERGAN** *Gregory Kern* 40p

R 41   **JAMES GUNN 1: THE DEADLY STRANGER**
                                                      John Delaney 40p

R 68   **CHURCHILL'S VIXENS 1: THE BRETON BUTCHER**
                                                   Leslie McManus 40p

R114   **CHURCHILL'S VIXENS 2: THE BELGIAN FOX**
                                                   Leslie McManus 40p

R 76   **THE BIG BRAIN 1: THE AARDVARK AFFAIR**
                                                   Gary Brandner 40p

R 84   **THE CRAFT OF TERROR** *Ed. Peter Haining* 40p

R122   **BLACK SCARAB** *Norman Gant* 40p

NEL P.O. BOX 11, FALMOUTH, TR10 9EN, CORNWALL.

For U.K.: Customers should include to cover postage, 18p for the first book plus 8p per copy for each additional book ordered up to a maximum charge of 66p.

For B.F.P.O. and Eire: Customers should include to cover postage, 18p for the first book plus 8p per copy for the next 6 and thereafter 3p per book.

For Overseas: Customers should include to cover postage, 20p for the first book plus 10p per copy for each additional book.

Name ....

Address ....

....

....

Title ....

Whilst every effort is made to maintain prices, new editions or printings may carry an increased price and the actual price of the edition supplied will apply.